Study Guide & Working Papers

for

College Accounting: A Contemporary Approach

Third Edition

M. David Haddock, Jr.
Chattanooga State Community College
Emeritus

John Ellis Price
University of North Texas

Michael J. Farina
Cerritos College

STUDY GUIDE & WORKING PAPERS FOR
COLLEGE ACCOUNTING: A CONTEMPORARY APPROACH, THIRD EDITION

Published by McGraw-Hill Education, 2 Penn Plaza, New York, NY 10121.

Some ancillaries, including electronic and print components, may not be available to customers outside the United States.

This book is printed on acid-free paper.

4 5 6 7 8 9 0 ROV/ROV 1 0 9 8 7 6 5

ISBN: 978-0-07-763978-5
MHID: 0-07-763978-2

www.mhhe.com

Table of Contents

CHAPTER 1

Accounting: The Language of Business

STUDY GUIDE

STUDY GUIDE

Understanding the Chapter

Objectives

1. Define accounting. **2.** Identify and discuss career opportunities in accounting. **3.** Identify the users of financial information. **4.** Compare and contrast the three types of business entities. **5.** Describe the process used to develop generally accepted accounting principles. **6.** Define the accounting terms new to this chapter.

Reading Assignment

Read Chapter 1 in the textbook. Complete the textbook Section Self Review as you finish reading each section of the chapter, and the Comprehensive Self Review at the end of the chapter. Refer to the Chapter 1 Glossary or to the Glossary at the end of the book to find definitions for terms that are not familiar to you.

Activities

- ❑ **Thinking Critically** — Answer the *Thinking Critically* questions for Google and Managerial Implications.
- ❑ **Discussion Questions** — Answer each assigned discussion question in Chapter 1.
- ❑ **Critical Thinking Problem** — Complete the critical thinking problem as assigned.
- ❑ **Business Connections** — Complete the Business Connections activities as assigned to gain a deeper understanding of Chapter 1 concepts.

Practice Tests

Complete the Practice Tests, which cover the main points in your reading assignment. Compare your answers with those in the Practice Test Answer Key for Chapter 1 at the end of this chapter. If you have answered any questions incorrectly, review the related section of the text.

Part A True-False *For each of the following statements, circle T in the answer column if the answer is true or F if the answer is false.*

T F 1. Because of the difference in the structures of the three types of business entities, certain aspects of their financial affairs are accounted for in different ways.

T F 2. A sole proprietorship is a form of business entity owned by two or more people.

T F 3. There is little difference between a corporation and other forms of business entities.

T F 4. Shares of stock represent ownership in a corporation.

T F 5. Employees should have no particular interest in the financial information about the business for which they work.

T F 6. The American Institute of Certified Public Accountants is a governmental agency.

T F 7. In a large company, the auditing process is completed by bookkeepers.

T F 8. Passing a test called the Uniform CPA Examination is required for one to become a certified public accountant.

T F 9. The Securities and Exchange Commission has a great deal of power to dictate accounting methods used by companies whose stock is traded on the stock exchanges.

T F 10. The Securities and Exchange Commission often relies on pronouncements of the Financial Accounting Standards Board.

T F 11. The Financial Accounting Standards Board issues income tax rules.

T F 12. Because of the separate entity assumption, the personal financial activities of the owner of a sole proprietorship are combined with the financial affairs of his or her business in the accounting records of the business.

T F 13. All accounting principles are established by law.

Part B Completion *In the answer column, supply the missing word or words needed to complete each of the following statements.*

Language of business **1.** Many people call accounting the ______ ______ ______.

International Accounting **2.** ______ ______ is the study of accounting principles used by different countries.

FBI **3.** The IRS and the ______ have large numbers of accountants on their staff and use them to uncover possible violations of the law.

Governmental Accounting **4.** Major areas of accounting are public accounting, managerial accounting, and ______ ______.

AAA **5.** The ______ is an organization of accounting educators.

AICPA **6.** The ______ is a national association of professional accountants.

General Accepted Acct. Princ **7.** ______ ______ ______ ______ are developed by the Financial Accounting Standards Board.

SEC **8.** The ______ was created to review and oversee the accounting methods of publicly owned corporations.

IRS **9.** The ______ and other tax authorities are interested in financial information about a firm.

Stockholders / Shareholders **10.** Corporate owners are called ______ ______.

Shares of Stock **11.** Ownership in a corporation is evidenced by ______ ___ ______.

partnership **12.** The three major types of business entities are sole proprietorships, corporations, and ______.

Social Entity **13.** An economic entity is an organization whose major purpose is to produce a profit, whereas a(n) ______ ______ is a nonprofit organization.

record or classifying **14.** The accounting process involves ______, ______, summarizing, interpreting, and communicating financial information about an economic or social entity.

financial Statements **15.** Periodic reports prepared from accounting records are called ______ ______.

WORKING PAPERS

Name

CRITICAL THINKING PROBLEM 1.1

Chapter 1 Practice Test Answer Key

Part A True-False

1. **T**
2. **F**
3. **F**
4. **T**
5. **F**
6. **F**
7. **F**
8. **T**
9. **T**
10. **T**
11. **F**
12. **F**
13. **F**

Part B Completion

1. language of business
2. International accounting
3. FBI
4. governmental accounting
5. AAA
6. AICPA
7. Generally accepted accounting principles
8. SEC
9. IRS
10. stockholders or shareholders
11. shares of stock
12. partnerships
13. social entity
14. recording, classifying
15. financial statements

CHAPTER 2 Analyzing Business Transactions

STUDY GUIDE

Understanding the Chapter

Objectives

1. Record in equation form the financial effects of a business transaction. **2.** Define, identify, and understand the relationship between asset, liability, and owner's equity accounts. **3.** Analyze the effects of business transactions on a firm's assets, liabilities, and owner's equity and record these effects in accounting equation form. **4.** Prepare an income statement. **5.** Prepare a statement of owner's equity and a balance sheet **6.** Define the accounting terms new to this chapter.

Reading Assignment

Read Chapter 2 in the textbook. Complete the textbook Section Self Review as you finish reading each section of the chapter, and the Comprehensive Self Review at the end of the chapter. Refer to the Chapter 2 Glossary or to the Glossary at the end of the book to find definitions for terms that are not familiar to you.

Activities

- ❑ **Thinking Critically** — Answer the *Thinking Critically* questions for Southwest Airlines and Managerial Implications.
- ❑ **Discussion Questions** — Answer each assigned discussion question in Chapter 2.
- ❑ **Exercises** — Complete each assigned exercise in Chapter 2. Use the forms provided in this SGWP. The objectives covered by an exercise are given after the exercise number. If you need help with an exercise, review the portion of the chapter related to the objective(s) covered.
- ❑ **Problems A/B** — Complete each assigned problem in Chapter 2. Use the forms provided in this SGWP. The objectives covered by a problem are given after the problem number. If you need help with a problem, review the portion of the chapter related to the objective(s) covered.
- ❑ **Critical Thinking Problems 2.1 and 2.2** — Complete Critical Thinking Problems 2.1 and 2.2 as assigned. Use the forms provided in this SGWP.
- ❑ **Business Connections** — Complete the Business Connections activities as assigned to gain a deeper understanding of Chapter 2 concepts.

Practice Tests

Complete the Practice Tests, which cover the main points in your reading assignment. Compare your answers with those in the Practice Test Answer Key for Chapter 2 at the end of this chapter. If you have answered any questions incorrectly, review the related section of the text.

Part A True-False *For each of the following statements, circle T in the answer column if the answer is true or F if the answer is false.*

(T) F 1. The balance sheet shows the financial position of a business on a specific date.

(T) F 2. A profit and loss statement is another name for the income statement.

T (F) 3. The balance sheet is prepared at the end of the accounting period to show the results of operations.

(T) F 4. A net loss results if total expenses exceed total revenue.

T (F) 5. The net income or net loss for the period is shown in the Assets section of the balance sheet.

(T) F 6. The net income or net loss for the period is shown on both the income statement and the statement of owner's equity.

T (F) 7. The collection of cash from accounts receivable increases owner's equity.

(T) F 8. Expenses decrease owner's equity.

T (F) 9. Revenue decreases owner's equity.

(T) F 10. When equipment is purchased for cash, there is no change in the total value of the firm's property.

Part B Matching *For each numbered item, choose the matching term from the box and write the identifying letter in the answer column.*

B 1. Property owned by a business.

F 2. A business obligation or debt.

E 3. Owner's financial interest in the business.

C 4. Those to whom money is owed.

H 5. An expression of the relationship in which assets equal liabilities plus owner's equity.

D 6. Inflows of money or other assets resulting from sales of goods or service.

G 7. Amount remaining when total revenue is more than total expenses.

A 8. Amounts owed by charge account customers.

a. Accounts Receivable
b. Assets
c. Creditors
d. Revenue
e. Owner's equity
f. Liability
g. Net income
h. Fundamental accounting equation

Part C Completion *In the answer column, supply the missing word or words needed to complete each of the following statements.*

Answer	Statement
Profit	**1.** The basic reason for starting a business is the possibility of making a ______.
credit or account	**2.** Accounts receivable result when goods are sold or services are performed on ______ __ ______.
reduced or decreased	**3.** When expenses are paid, the owner's equity is ______.
assets	**4.** Regardless of the number and variety of transactions, liabilities plus owner's equity always equal ______.
asset or property	**5.** When supplies are first purchased for use in operations, they are considered a type of ______.
equal	**6.** When property values and financial interest increase or decrease, the sum of the items on both sides of the equation always remains ______.
A/P or Liability	**7.** The purchase of new equipment on account creates a debt that is called a(n) ______ ______ or ______.
analyze	**8.** Accountants must ______ each business transaction before they can intelligently record, report, and interpret it.

Demonstration Problem

The account balances for Eugene Henderson, CPA, for the month of January 2016 are shown below in random order.

Rent Expense	$ 9,000	Advertising Expense	$ 7,250
Fees Earned	145,200	Office Equipment	58,640
Accounts Payable	30,440	T. Neal, Drawing	18,000
Salaries Expense	25,800	Accounts Receivable	32,475
Cash	190,674	E. Henderson, Capital 1/1	?

Instructions

1. Determine the balance for **Eugene Henderson, Capital,** on January 1, 2016.
2. Prepare an income statement, a statement of owner's equity, and a balance sheet as of January 31, 2016.
3. List the expenses on the income statement in alphabetical order.

SOLUTION

Determine the balance for Eugene Henderson Capital, on January 1, 2016.
Let Thomas Neal, Capital = X. Solving for X:

Assets						=	Liabilities	+	Owner's Equity						
		Accts.		Office			Accounts		E. Henderson						
Cash	+	Rec.	+	Equip.		=	Payable	+	Capital	−	Drawing	+	Revenue	−	Expenses
190,674	+	32,475	+	58,640		=	30,440	+	X	−	18,000	+	145,200	−	42,050
				281,789		=	115,590	+	X						
		281,789	−	115,590		=	115,590	−	115,590	+	X				
				166,199		=	X								

Thomas Neal, Capital, January 1, 2013 = **$166,199**

Total Expenses:

Rent Expense	$ 9,000
Salaries Expense	25,800
Advertising Expense	7,250
	$42,050

Eugene Henderson, CPA
Income Statement
Month Ended January 31, 2016

Revenue		
Fees Earned		145 200 00
Expenses		
Rent Expense	9 000 00	
Salaries Expense	25 800 00	
Advertising Expense	7 250 00	
Total Expenses		42 050 00
Net Income		103 150 00

Eugene Henderson, CPA
Statement of Owner's Equity
Month Ended January 31, 2016

Eugene Henderson, Capital, January 1, 2016		166 199 00
Net Income	103 150 00	
Less Withdrawals	18 000 00	
Increase in Capital		85 150 00
Eugene Henderson, Capital, January 31, 2016		251 349 00

SOLUTION (continued)

Eugene Henderson, CPA
Balance Sheet
January 31, 2016

Assets		Liabilities	
Cash	190,674.00	Accounts Payable	30,440.00
Accounts Receivable	32,475.00	**Owner's Equity**	
Office Equipment	58,640.00	Eugene Henderson, Capital	251,349.00
Total Assets	281,789.00	Total Liabilities and Owner's Equity	281,789.00

WORKING PAPERS

Name ______________________

EXERCISE 2.1

Assets ______________________

Liabilities ______________________

Owner's Equity ______________________

EXERCISE 2.2

1. ______________________

2. ______________________

3. ______________________

4. ______________________

5. ______________________

EXERCISE 2.3

	Assets	=	Liabilities	+	Owner's Equity
1.		=		+	
2.		=		+	
3.		=		+	
4.		=		+	
5.		=		+	

EXERCISE 2.4

Transaction	Assets	=	Liabilities	+	Owner's Equity
1.	+	=		+	+
2.		=		+	
3.		=		+	
4.		=		+	
5.		=		+	

Name ______________________

EXERCISE 2.5

	Assets			=	Liabilities	+	Owner's Equity		
	Cash	+ Accounts Receivable	+ Equipment	=	Accounts Payable	+	Amos Roberts Capital	+ Revenue	− Expenses
1.									
2.									
3.									
4.									
5.									
6.									
7.									
8.									
Totals		+	+	=		+		+	−

EXERCISE 2.6

Revenue

Expenses

EXERCISE 2.7

1.
2.
3.
4.
5.
6.
7.

Name

EXERCISE 2.8

EXERCISE 2.9

Revenue

Expenses

Name

EXERCISE 2.10

Name ______________________

PROBLEM 2.1A or 2.1B

	Assets				=	Liabilities	+	Owner's Equity
	Cash	+ Accounts Receivable	+ Supplies	+ Equipment	=	Accounts Payable	+	Owner's Capital
1.								
2.								
3.								
4.								
5.								
6.								
7.								
8.								
9.								
10.								
11.								
Totals		+	+	+	=		+	

Analyze: ______________________

Name ______________________________

PROBLEM 2.2A or 2.2B

	Assets				=	Liabilities	+	Owner's Equity		
	Cash	+ Accounts Receivable	+	+	=	Accounts Payable	+	Capital	+ Revenue	− Expenses
Beginning Balances	+	+	+		=	+		+	−	
1.										
New Balances	+	+	+		=	+		+	−	
2.										
New Balances	+	+	+		=	+		+	−	
3.										
New Balances	+	+	+		=	+		+	−	
4.										
New Balances	+	+	+		=	+		+	−	
5.										
New Balances	+	+	+		=	+		+	−	
6.										
New Balances	+	+	+		=	+		+	−	
7.										
New Balances	+	+	+		=	+		+	−	
8.										
New Balances	+	+	+		=	+		+	−	
9.										
New Balances	+	+	+		=	+		+	−	
10.										
New Balances	+	+	+		=	+		+	−	

Analyze: ______________________________

Name

PROBLEM 2.3A or 2.3B

Analyze:

PROBLEM 2.4A or 2.4B

Name

PROBLEM 2.4A or 2.4B (continued)

Analyze:

Name ______________________

CRITICAL THINKING PROBLEM 2.1

Determine the balance for **Carl Nicholson**, April 30, 2016.

Assets			= Liabilities +	Owner's Equity			
Cash	+ Accounts Receivable	+ Machinery	= Accounts Payable	+ D. Garcia Capital	− D. Garcia Drawing	+ Revenue	− Expenses
$30,000	+ $12,000	+ $21,000	= $13,200	+ ?	− $6,800	+ $26,800	− $21,490

Let Carl Nicholson, Capital = X.

Solving for X:

Carl Nicholson, Capital, April 1, 2016,= ______

Advertising Expense	$ 3,890
Maintenance Expense	4,600
Salaries Expense	13,000
Total Expenses	

Name ______________________________

CRITICAL THINKING PROBLEM 2.1 (continued)

Analyze: ______________________________

Chapter 2 Practice Test Answer Key

Part A True-False

1.	**T**	**6.**	**T**
2.	**T**	**7.**	**F**
3.	**F**	**8.**	**T**
4.	**T**	**9.**	**F**
5.	**F**	**10.**	**T**

Part B Matching

1.	**b**	**5.**	**h**
2.	**f**	**6.**	**d**
3.	**e**	**7.**	**g**
4.	**c**	**8.**	**a**

Part C Completion

1. profit
2. credit or on account
3. reduced or decreased
4. assets
5. asset or property
6. equal
7. accounts payable or liability
8. analyze

Name

CRITICAL THINKING PROBLEM 2.2

CHAPTER 3

Analyzing Business Transactions Using T Accounts

STUDY GUIDE

Understanding the Chapter

Objectives

1. Set up T accounts for assets, liabilities, and owner's equity. **2.** Analyze business transactions and enter them in the accounts. **3.** Determine the balance of an account. **4.** Set up T accounts for revenue and expenses. **5.** Prepare a trial balance from T accounts. **6.** Prepare an income statement, a statement of owner's equity, and a balance sheet. **7.** Develop a chart of accounts. **8.** Define the accounting terms new to this chapter.

Reading Assignment

Read Chapter 3 in the textbook. Complete the textbook Section Self Review as you finish reading each section of the chapter, and the Comprehensive Self Review at the end of the chapter. Refer to the Chapter 3 Glossary or to the Glossary at the end of the book to find definitions for terms that are not familiar to you.

Activities

- ❑ **Thinking Critically** — Answer the *Thinking Critically* questions for AT&T and Managerial Implications.
- ❑ **Discussion Questions** — Answer each assigned discussion question in Chapter 3.
- ❑ **Exercises** — Complete each assigned exercise in Chapter 3. Use the forms provided in this SGWP. The objectives covered by an exercise are given after the exercise number. If you need help with an exercise, review the portion of the chapter related to the objective(s) covered.
- ❑ **Problems A/B** — Complete each assigned problem in Chapter 3. Use the forms provided in this SGWP. The objectives covered by a problem are given after the problem number. If you need help with a problem, review the portion of the chapter related to the objective(s) covered.
- ❑ **Critical Thinking Problems** — Complete the critical thinking problems as assigned. Use the forms provided in this SGWP.
- ❑ **Business Connections** — Complete the Business Connections activities as assigned to gain a deeper understanding of Chapter 3 concepts.

Practice Tests

Complete the Practice Tests, which cover the main points in your reading assignment. Compare your answers with those in the Practice Test Answer Key for Chapter 3 at the end of this chapter. If you have answered any questions incorrectly, review the related section of the text.

Part A True-False *For each of the following statements, circle T in the answer column if the answer is true or F if the answer is false.*

(T)	F	1. An entry on the left side of any account is called a debit.
(T)	F	2. Revenue accounts are increased by credits.
T	(F)	3. Decreases in liabilities are credited to the liability account.
T	(F)	4. Increases in liabilities are recorded on the debit side of an account.
T	(F)	5. Decreases in assets are recorded on the left side of an account.
(T)	F	6. Increases in assets are recorded on the debit side of an account.
T	(F)	7. Increases in expense accounts are recorded by credit entries.
T	(F)	8. The owner's beginning investment is entered as a debit in the owner's capital account.
(T)	F	9. The **Accounts Payable** account is decreased by a debit entry.
T	(F)	10. A cash payment by a business is recorded as a debit entry in the **Cash** account.
(T)	F	11. The receipt of cash is recorded by a debit entry to the **Cash** account.
(T)	F	12. A reduction in the equity of the owner is recorded by making a debit entry in the **Owner's Drawing** account.
(T)	F	13. Accountants keep a separate record for each asset, liability, and owner's equity item.
(T)	F	14. The T account allows increases and decreases to be separated and recorded on different sides.
(T)	F	15. An increase in the owner's investment is recorded by crediting the owner's capital account.

Part B Matching *For each numbered item, choose the matching item from the box and write the identifying letter in the answer column.*

a. Account	**f.** Expense
b. Double-entry system	**g.** Revenue
c. Credit	**h.** Chart of accounts
d. Permanent accounts	**i.** Debit
e. Temporary accounts	

i **1.** An entry on the left side of an account.

c **2.** An entry on the right side of an account.

h **3.** A system for arranging accounts in logical order.

f **4.** An operating cost that decreases owner's equity.

b **5.** The system of accounting that requires equality of the entries on each side of the equation.

d **6.** Accounts whose balances are carried forward to start a new period.

e **7.** Accounts whose balances are transferred to a summary account at the end of the accounting period.

g **8.** A subdivision of owner's equity that is used to record various types of income of a business.

a **9.** A separate written record that is kept for each asset, liability, and owner's equity item.

Part C Completion *In the answer column, supply the missing word or words needed to complete each of the following statements.*

trial balance **1.** The ______ ______ is a statement prepared to test the accuracy of the figures recorded in the accounts.

Normal Balance **2.** The ______ ______ of an account is where increases in the account are recorded and where the balance is recorded.

footing **3.** A(n) ______ is the total of several entries on either side of an account that is entered in small pencil.

transposition **4.** A(n) ______ is an error where the digits of a number are switched.

slide **5.** A(n) ______ is an error where the decimal point is misplaced.

Demonstration Problem

Anita Thomas is an investment broker who operates her own business, Thomas Investment Counseling.

Instructions

1. Analyze the transactions for the month of January 2016, and record each in the appropriate T accounts. Use plus and minus signs to show increases and decreases. Identify each entry in the T accounts by writing the number of the transaction next to the entry.
2. Determine the balance for each T account. Prepare a trial balance.

Transactions

1. Anita Thomas invested $100,000 in cash to start the business.
2. Thomas Investment Counseling purchased office furniture for $20,000 on account.
3. Paid $7,500 for one month's rent.
4. Sold an investment portfolio to the Darden Family and received fees of $75,000.
5. Purchased a computer for $2,500, paying $1,250 in cash and putting the balance on account for 60 days.
6. Paid $10,200 for employee salaries.
7. Purchased office equipment for $16,800 with credit terms of 60 days.
8. Sold an investment portfolio to the Williams Family and will receive commission fees of $30,900 in 30 days.
9. Issued a check for $6,800 for partial payment of the amount for office equipment.
10. Anita Thomas withdrew $7,500 in cash for personal use.
11. Issued a check for $1,560 to pay the utility bill.

SOLUTION

Cash

(1)	+ 100,000	(3)	− 7,500
(4)	+ 75,000	(5)	− 1,250
		(6)	− 10,200
		(9)	− 6,800
	175,000	(10)	− 7,500
		(11)	− 1,560
Bal.	140,190		34,810

Accounts Receivable

(8)	+ 30,900		

Office Furniture

(2)	+ 20,000		

Office Equipment

(5)	+ 2,500		
(7)	+ 16,800		
Bal.	19,300		

Accounts Payable

(9)	− 6,800	(2)	+ 20,000
		(5)	+ 1,250
		(7)	+ 16,800
		Bal.	31,250

Anita Thomas, Capital

		(1)	+ 100,000

Anita Thomas, Drawing

(10)	+ 7,500		

Fees Income

		(4)	+ 75,000
		(8)	+ 30,900
		Bal.	105,900

Rent Expense

(3)	+ 7,500		

Salaries Expense

(6)	+ 10,200		

Utilities Expense

(11)	+ 1,560		

SOLUTION (continued)

Thomas Investment Counseling
Trial Balance
January 31, 2016

ACCOUNT NAME	DEBIT	CREDIT
Cash	140 1 9 0 00	
Accounts Receivable	30 9 0 0 00	
Office Furniture	20 0 0 0 00	
Office Equipment	19 3 0 0 00	
Accounts Payable		31 2 5 0 00
Anita Thomas, Capital		100 0 0 0 00
Anita Thomas, Drawing	7 5 0 0 00	
Fees Income		105 9 0 0 00
Rent Expense	7 5 0 0 00	
Salaries Expense	10 2 0 0 00	
Utilities Expense	1 5 6 0 00	
Totals	237 1 5 0 00	237 1 5 0 00

WORKING PAPERS

Name ______________________________

EXERCISE 3.1

EXERCISE 3.2

EXERCISE 3.3

1. ______________________________
2. ______________________________
3. ______________________________
4. ______________________________
5. ______________________________
6. ______________________________
7. ______________________________
8. ______________________________

Name ______________________

EXERCISE 3.4

1. ______________________
2. ______________________
3. ______________________
4. ______________________
5. ______________________

EXERCISE 3.5

EXERCISE 3.6

ACCOUNT NAME	DEBIT	CREDIT

Name

EXERCISE 3.6 (continued)

EXERCISE 3.7

Name

EXERCISE 3.7 (continued)

EXERCISE 3.8

Name ______________________

PROBLEM 3.1A or 3.1B

1.

2.

3.

4.

5.

6.

7.

8.

Analyze: ______________________

PROBLEM 3.2A or 3.2B

1.

2.

3.

4.

5.

6.

7.

8.

Analyze: ______________________

Name

PROBLEM 3.3A or 3.3B

1.

2.

3.

4.

5.

6.

7.

8.

9.

10.

11.

12.

Name ____________________

PROBLEM 3.4A or 3.4B

Analyze: ____________________

Name

PROBLEM 3.5A or 3.5B

ACCOUNT NAME	DEBIT	CREDIT

Name

PROBLEM 3.5A or 3.5B (continued)

Analyze:

Name

CRITICAL THINKING PROBLEM 3.1

Name

CRITICAL THINKING PROBLEM 3.1 (continued)

Name

CRITICAL THINKING PROBLEM 3.1 (continued)

Name

CRITICAL THINKING PROBLEM 3.2

Name

CRITICAL THINKING PROBLEM 3.2 (continued)

ACCOUNT NAME	DEBIT	CREDIT

Name

CRITICAL THINKING PROBLEM 3.2 (continued)

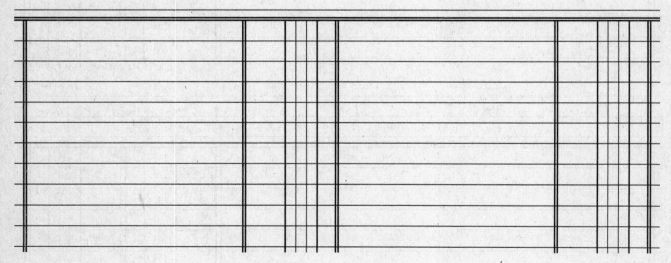

Analyze:

Chapter 3 Practice Test Answer Key

Part A True-False

1. T	**6.** T	**11.** T
2. T	**7.** F	**12.** T
3. F	**8.** F	**13.** T
4. F	**9.** T	**14.** T
5. F	**10.** F	**15.** T

Part B Matching

1. i	**6.** d
2. c	**7.** e
3. h	**8.** g
4. f	**9.** a
5. b	

Part C Completion

1. trial balance
2. normal balance
3. footing
4. transposition
5. slide

CHAPTER 4

The General Journal and the General Ledger

STUDY GUIDE

STUDY GUIDE

Understanding the Chapter

Objectives

1. Record transactions in the general journal. **2.** Prepare compound journal entries. **3.** Post journal entries to general ledger accounts. **4.** Correct errors made in the journal or ledger. **5.** Define the accounting terms new to this chapter.

Reading Assignment

Read Chapter 4 in the textbook. Complete the textbook Section Self Review as you finish reading each section of the chapter, and the Comprehensive Self Review at the end of the chapter. Refer to the Chapter 4 Glossary or to the Glossary at the end of the book to find definitions for terms that are not familiar to you.

Activities

- ❑ **Thinking Critically** — Answer the *Thinking Critically* questions for Boeing and Managerial Implications.
- ❑ **Discussion Questions** — Answer each assigned discussion question in Chapter 4.
- ❑ **Exercises** — Complete each assigned exercise in Chapter 4. Use the forms provided in this SGWP. The objectives covered by an exercise are given after the exercise number. If you need help with an exercise, review the portion of the chapter related to the objective(s) covered.
- ❑ **Problems A/B** — Complete each assigned problem in Chapter 4. Use the forms provided in this SGWP. The objectives covered by a problem are given after the problem number. If you need help with a problem, review the portion of the chapter related to the objective(s) covered.
- ❑ **Critical Thinking Problems** — Complete the critical thinking problems as assigned. Use the forms provided in this SGWP.
- ❑ **Business Connections** — Complete the Business Connections activities as assigned to gain a deeper understanding of Chapter 4 concepts.

Practice Tests

Complete the Practice Tests, which cover the main points in your reading assignment. Compare your answers with those in the Practice Test Answer Key for Chapter 4 at the end of this chapter. If you have answered any questions incorrectly, review the related section of the text.

Part A Matching *For each numbered item, choose the matching term from the box and write the identifying letter in the answer column.*

a. journal
b. source documents
c. posting
d. general ledger
e. T accounts
f. journalizing
g. correcting entry
h. compound entry
i. balance ledger form
j. audit trail

A ___ **1.** Record of original entry.

F ___ **2.** The process of recording transactions in the journal.

B ___ **3.** Invoices and other business forms that contain the original data about transactions.

J ___ **4.** A chain of references that makes it possible to trace information about transactions through an accounting system.

I ___ **5.** A ledger account form that always shows the current balance of an account.

H ___ **6.** A journal entry that consists of more than one debit or more than one credit.

D ___ **7.** A permanent, classified record of all accounts used by a business.

E ___ **8.** Used to analyze transactions but not used to maintain financial records.

C ___ **9.** The process of transferring information from the journal to the ledger.

G ___ **10.** An entry that is made when there is an error in data that has been journalized and posted.

Part B Completion *In the answer column, supply the missing word or words needed to complete each of the following statements.*

Ledger ___ **1.** All the accounts together constitute a(n) ______, or a record of final entry.

Posting Refrence ___ **2.** Notations that allow the data in journals and ledgers to be easily traced are called ______ ______.

Brief or Concise ___ **3.** Descriptions in the general journal should be complete but ______ ______ ______.

Credit ___ **4.** On the balance ledger form the second money column is used to record ______ amounts.

debit ___ **5.** On the balance ledger form the first money column is used to record ______ amounts.

Debit ___ **6.** The accountant always records the ______ items first in the Description column of the journal.

year ___ **7.** The ______ is always entered at the top of the Date column.

Chronological or date ___ **8.** The accountant enters transactions in the general journal in ______ or ______ order.

assets or Balance Sheet account ___ **9.** The pages in the ledger are usually organized so that the ______ or ______ ______ ______ come first.

Posted ___ **10.** If an error is discovered in a journal before the entry is ______, the error can be neatly crossed out and the correct data written above it.

Demonstration Problem

On January 1, 2016, Herschel Anderson opened his consulting office and began business as Anderson Consulting Services. Selected transactions for the first month of operations follow.

Instructions

1. Journalize the transactions on page 1 of a general journal. Write the year at the top of the Date column; include an explanation for each entry.
2. Post to the general ledger accounts. Use account numbers from accounts in working papers in General Ledger.
3. Prepare a trial balance.

DATE	TRANSACTIONS
January 1	Herschel Anderson invested $120,000 cash in the business.
2	Issued Check 101 for $7,500 to pay the January rent.
5	Purchased office equipment for $38,000 from Oxford Office Supply, Invoice 7045; issued Check 102 for $18,000 down payment with the balance due in 30 days.
12	Wrote a lease contract for Neal Davis for $7,000 cash.
15	Performed consulting services for a client, Williams Supply Company, for $25,000 to be received in 30 days.
28	Issued Check 103 for $12,000 for payment to Oxford Office Supply.
29	Issued Check 104 for $15,000 to Herschel Anderson for personal use.
31	Received $15,000 from Williams Supply Company for partial payment of its account.

SOLUTION

GENERAL JOURNAL PAGE 1

DATE		DESCRIPTION	POST. REF.	DEBIT	CREDIT
2016					
Jan.	1	Cash	101	120,000.00	
		Herschel Anderson Capital	301		120,000.00
		Investment to start business			
	2	Rent Expense	514	7,500.00	
		Cash	101		7,500.00
		Issued Check 101 for January rent			
	5	Office Equipment	131	38,000.00	
		Cash	101		18,000.00
		Accounts Payable	202		20,000.00
		Issued Check 102 for office equipment,			
		balance due in 30 days.			
	12	Cash	101	7,000.00	
		Fees Income	401		7,000.00
		Performed services for cash.			
	15	Accounts Receivable	111	25,000.00	
		Fees Income	401		25,000.00
		Performed services on account.			
	28	Accounts Payable	202	12,000.00	
		Cash	101		12,000.00
		Paid Invoice 7045, Check 103			
	29	Herschel Anderson, Drawing	302	15,000.00	
		Cash	101		15,000.00
		Issued Check 104 to owner for personal use.			
	31	Cash	101	15,000.00	
		Accounts Receivable	111		15,000.00
		Received partial payment			
		from Williams Supply Company			

SOLUTION (continued)

GENERAL LEDGER

ACCOUNT **Cash** ACCOUNT NO. **101**

DATE		DESCRIPTION	POST. REF.	DEBIT	CREDIT	BALANCE DEBIT	BALANCE CREDIT
2016							
Jan.	**1**		**J1**	**120 0 0 0 00**		**120 0 0 0 00**	
	2		**J1**		**7 5 0 0 00**	**112 5 0 0 00**	
	5		**J1**		**18 0 0 0 00**	**94 5 0 0 00**	
	12		**J1**	**7 0 0 0 00**		**101 5 0 0 00**	
	28		**J1**		**12 0 0 0 00**	**89 5 0 0 00**	
	29		**J1**		**15 0 0 0 00**	**74 5 0 0 00**	
	31		**J1**	**15 0 0 0 00**		**89 5 0 0 00**	

ACCOUNT **Accounts Receivable** ACCOUNT NO. **111**

DATE		DESCRIPTION	POST. REF.	DEBIT	CREDIT	BALANCE DEBIT	BALANCE CREDIT
2016							
Jan.	**15**		**J1**	**25 0 0 0 00**		**25 0 0 0 00**	
	31		**J1**		**15 0 0 0 00**	**10 0 0 0 00**	

ACCOUNT **Office Equipment** ACCOUNT NO. **131**

DATE		DESCRIPTION	POST. REF.	DEBIT	CREDIT	BALANCE DEBIT	BALANCE CREDIT
2016							
Jan.	**5**		**J1**	**38 0 0 0 00**		**38 0 0 0 00**	

ACCOUNT **Accounts Payable** ACCOUNT NO. **202**

DATE		DESCRIPTION	POST. REF.	DEBIT	CREDIT	BALANCE DEBIT	BALANCE CREDIT
2016							
Jan.	**5**		**J1**		**20 0 0 0 00**		**20 0 0 0 00**
	28		**J1**	**12 0 0 0 00**			**8 0 0 0 00**

ACCOUNT **Herschel Anderson, Capital** ACCOUNT NO. **301**

DATE		DESCRIPTION	POST. REF.	DEBIT	CREDIT	BALANCE DEBIT	BALANCE CREDIT
2016							
Jan.	**1**		**J1**		**120 0 0 0 00**		**120 0 0 0 00**

SOLUTION (continued)

ACCOUNT **Herschel Anderson, Drawing** ACCOUNT NO. **302**

DATE		DESCRIPTION	POST. REF.	DEBIT	CREDIT	BALANCE DEBIT	BALANCE CREDIT
2016							
Jan.	**29**		**J1**	**15 0 0 0 00**		**15 0 0 0 00**	

ACCOUNT **Fees Income** ACCOUNT NO. **401**

DATE		DESCRIPTION	POST. REF.	DEBIT	CREDIT	BALANCE DEBIT	BALANCE CREDIT
2016							
Jan.	**12**		**J1**		**7 0 0 0 00**		**7 0 0 0 00**
	15		**J1**		**25 0 0 0 00**		**32 0 0 0 00**

ACCOUNT **Rent Expense** ACCOUNT NO. **514**

DATE		DESCRIPTION	POST. REF.	DEBIT	CREDIT	BALANCE DEBIT	BALANCE CREDIT
2016							
Jan.	**2**		**J1**	**7 5 0 0 00**		**7 5 0 0 00**	

Anderson Consulting Services

Trial Balance

January 31, 2016

ACCOUNT NAME	DEBIT	CREDIT
Cash	**89 5 0 0 00**	
Accounts Receivable	**10 0 0 0 00**	
Office Equipment	**38 0 0 0 00**	
Accounts Payable		**8 0 0 0 00**
Herschel Anderson, Capital		**120 0 0 0 00**
Herschel Anderson, Drawing	**15 0 0 0 00**	
Fees Income		**32 0 0 0 00**
Rent Expense	**7 5 0 0 00**	
Totals	**160 0 0 0 00**	**160 0 0 0 00**

WORKING PAPERS

Name ______________________

EXERCISE 4.1

	Debit	Credit		Debit	Credit		Debit	Credit
1.			5.			8.		
2.			6.			9.		
3.			7.			10.		
4.								

EXERCISE 4.2

GENERAL JOURNAL

PAGE ______

DATE	DESCRIPTION	POST. REF.	DEBIT	CREDIT

Name ____________________

EXERCISE 4.2 (continued)

GENERAL JOURNAL　　　　PAGE ______

	DATE	DESCRIPTION	POST. REF.	DEBIT	CREDIT	
1						1
2						2
3						3
4						4
5						5
6						6
7						7
8						8
9						9
10						10
11						11
12						12
13						13
14						14
15						15
16						16

EXERCISE 4.3

GENERAL LEDGER

ACCOUNT ____________________　　ACCOUNT NO. ______

DATE	DESCRIPTION	POST. REF.	DEBIT	CREDIT	BALANCE	
					DEBIT	CREDIT

Name ______________________

EXERCISE 4.3 (continued)

GENERAL LEDGER

ACCOUNT ______________________ ACCOUNT NO. ______

DATE	DESCRIPTION	POST. REF.	DEBIT	CREDIT	BALANCE DEBIT	BALANCE CREDIT

ACCOUNT ______________________ ACCOUNT NO. ______

DATE	DESCRIPTION	POST. REF.	DEBIT	CREDIT	BALANCE DEBIT	BALANCE CREDIT

ACCOUNT ______________________ ACCOUNT NO. ______

DATE	DESCRIPTION	POST. REF.	DEBIT	CREDIT	BALANCE DEBIT	BALANCE CREDIT

ACCOUNT ______________________ ACCOUNT NO. ______

DATE	DESCRIPTION	POST. REF.	DEBIT	CREDIT	BALANCE DEBIT	BALANCE CREDIT

ACCOUNT ______________________ ACCOUNT NO. ______

DATE	DESCRIPTION	POST. REF.	DEBIT	CREDIT	BALANCE DEBIT	BALANCE CREDIT

Name

EXERCISE 4.3 (continued)

GENERAL LEDGER

ACCOUNT ______ ACCOUNT NO. ______

DATE		DESCRIPTION	POST. REF.	DEBIT	CREDIT	BALANCE DEBIT	BALANCE CREDIT

ACCOUNT ______ ACCOUNT NO. ______

DATE		DESCRIPTION	POST. REF.	DEBIT	CREDIT	BALANCE DEBIT	BALANCE CREDIT

ACCOUNT ______ ACCOUNT NO. ______

DATE		DESCRIPTION	POST. REF.	DEBIT	CREDIT	BALANCE DEBIT	BALANCE CREDIT

ACCOUNT ______ ACCOUNT NO. ______

DATE		DESCRIPTION	POST. REF.	DEBIT	CREDIT	BALANCE DEBIT	BALANCE CREDIT

ACCOUNT ______ ACCOUNT NO. ______

DATE		DESCRIPTION	POST. REF.	DEBIT	CREDIT	BALANCE DEBIT	BALANCE CREDIT

ACCOUNT ______ ACCOUNT NO. ______

DATE		DESCRIPTION	POST. REF.	DEBIT	CREDIT	BALANCE DEBIT	BALANCE CREDIT

Name

EXERCISE 4.4

GENERAL JOURNAL

PAGE

DATE		DESCRIPTION	POST. REF.	DEBIT	CREDIT

Name

EXERCISE 4.5

GENERAL JOURNAL

PAGE

DATE		DESCRIPTION	POST. REF.	DEBIT	CREDIT

EXERCISE 4.6

GENERAL JOURNAL

PAGE

DATE		DESCRIPTION	POST. REF.	DEBIT	CREDIT

EXTRA FORM

GENERAL JOURNAL

PAGE

DATE		DESCRIPTION	POST. REF.	DEBIT	CREDIT

Name

PROBLEM 4.1A or 4.1B

GENERAL JOURNAL

PAGE

DATE		DESCRIPTION	POST. REF.	DEBIT	CREDIT

Name ____________________

PROBLEM 4.1A or 4.1B (continued)

GENERAL JOURNAL

PAGE ______

DATE	DESCRIPTION	POST. REF.	DEBIT	CREDIT

Analyze: ____________________

Name ______________________

PROBLEM 4.2A or 4.2B

GENERAL JOURNAL

PAGE ________

DATE		DESCRIPTION	POST. REF.	DEBIT	CREDIT

Name

PROBLEM 4.2A or 4.2B (continued)

GENERAL JOURNAL

PAGE

DATE	DESCRIPTION	POST. REF.	DEBIT	CREDIT

Name

PROBLEM 4.2A or 4.2B (continued)

GENERAL LEDGER

ACCOUNT ______ ACCOUNT NO. ______

DATE	DESCRIPTION	POST. REF.	DEBIT	CREDIT	BALANCE DEBIT	BALANCE CREDIT

ACCOUNT ______ ACCOUNT NO. ______

DATE	DESCRIPTION	POST. REF.	DEBIT	CREDIT	BALANCE DEBIT	BALANCE CREDIT

ACCOUNT ______ ACCOUNT NO. ______

DATE	DESCRIPTION	POST. REF.	DEBIT	CREDIT	BALANCE DEBIT	BALANCE CREDIT

ACCOUNT ______ ACCOUNT NO. ______

DATE	DESCRIPTION	POST. REF.	DEBIT	CREDIT	BALANCE DEBIT	BALANCE CREDIT

Name ____________________

PROBLEM 4.2A or 4.2B (continued)

GENERAL LEDGER

ACCOUNT ____________________ ACCOUNT NO. ________

DATE		DESCRIPTION	POST. REF.	DEBIT	CREDIT	BALANCE DEBIT	BALANCE CREDIT

ACCOUNT ____________________ ACCOUNT NO. ________

DATE		DESCRIPTION	POST. REF.	DEBIT	CREDIT	BALANCE DEBIT	BALANCE CREDIT

ACCOUNT ____________________ ACCOUNT NO. ________

DATE		DESCRIPTION	POST. REF.	DEBIT	CREDIT	BALANCE DEBIT	BALANCE CREDIT

ACCOUNT ____________________ ACCOUNT NO. ________

DATE		DESCRIPTION	POST. REF.	DEBIT	CREDIT	BALANCE DEBIT	BALANCE CREDIT

ACCOUNT ____________________ ACCOUNT NO. ________

DATE		DESCRIPTION	POST. REF.	DEBIT	CREDIT	BALANCE DEBIT	BALANCE CREDIT

Name ______________________

PROBLEM 4.2A or 4.2B (continued)

GENERAL LEDGER

ACCOUNT ______________________ ACCOUNT NO. ________

DATE		DESCRIPTION	POST. REF.	DEBIT	CREDIT	BALANCE DEBIT	BALANCE CREDIT

ACCOUNT ______________________ ACCOUNT NO. ________

DATE		DESCRIPTION	POST. REF.	DEBIT	CREDIT	BALANCE DEBIT	BALANCE CREDIT

ACCOUNT ______________________ ACCOUNT NO. ________

DATE		DESCRIPTION	POST. REF.	DEBIT	CREDIT	BALANCE DEBIT	BALANCE CREDIT

ACCOUNT ______________________ ACCOUNT NO. ________

DATE		DESCRIPTION	POST. REF.	DEBIT	CREDIT	BALANCE DEBIT	BALANCE CREDIT

ACCOUNT ______________________ ACCOUNT NO. ________

DATE		DESCRIPTION	POST. REF.	DEBIT	CREDIT	BALANCE DEBIT	BALANCE CREDIT

Analyze: ______________________

Name ______________________

PROBLEM 4.3A or 4.3B

____

____

____

____

____

____

Analyze: ______________________

____

PROBLEM 4.4A or 4.4B

GENERAL JOURNAL PAGE ______

	DATE		DESCRIPTION	POST. REF.	DEBIT	CREDIT	
1							1
2							2
3							3
4							4
5							5
6							6
7							7
8							8
9							9
10							10
11							11
12							12
13							13
14							14
15							15
16							16
17							17
18							18
19							19
20							20
21							21
22							22
23							23
24							24
25							25
26							26

Name ______________________

PROBLEM 4.4A or 4.4B (continued)

GENERAL LEDGER

ACCOUNT ______________________ ACCOUNT NO. ______

DATE		DESCRIPTION	POST. REF.	DEBIT	CREDIT	BALANCE	
						DEBIT	CREDIT

ACCOUNT ______________________ ACCOUNT NO. ______

DATE		DESCRIPTION	POST. REF.	DEBIT	CREDIT	BALANCE	
						DEBIT	CREDIT

ACCOUNT ______________________ ACCOUNT NO. ______

DATE		DESCRIPTION	POST. REF.	DEBIT	CREDIT	BALANCE	
						DEBIT	CREDIT

ACCOUNT ______________________ ACCOUNT NO. ______

DATE		DESCRIPTION	POST. REF.	DEBIT	CREDIT	BALANCE	
						DEBIT	CREDIT

ACCOUNT ______________________ ACCOUNT NO. ______

DATE		DESCRIPTION	POST. REF.	DEBIT	CREDIT	BALANCE	
						DEBIT	CREDIT

Name ______________________

PROBLEM 4.4A or 4.4B (continued)

GENERAL LEDGER

ACCOUNT ______________________ ACCOUNT NO. ______

DATE	DESCRIPTION	POST. REF.	DEBIT	CREDIT	BALANCE DEBIT	BALANCE CREDIT

ACCOUNT ______________________ ACCOUNT NO. ______

DATE	DESCRIPTION	POST. REF.	DEBIT	CREDIT	BALANCE DEBIT	BALANCE CREDIT

ACCOUNT ______________________ ACCOUNT NO. ______

DATE	DESCRIPTION	POST. REF.	DEBIT	CREDIT	BALANCE DEBIT	BALANCE CREDIT

ACCOUNT ______________________ ACCOUNT NO. ______

DATE	DESCRIPTION	POST. REF.	DEBIT	CREDIT	BALANCE DEBIT	BALANCE CREDIT

Analyze: ______________________

EXTRA FORM

GENERAL LEDGER

ACCOUNT ______________________ ACCOUNT NO. ______

DATE	DESCRIPTION	POST. REF.	DEBIT	CREDIT	BALANCE DEBIT	BALANCE CREDIT

Name

CRITICAL THINKING PROBLEM 4.1

Name

CRITICAL THINKING PROBLEM 4.1 (continued)

Name ____________________

CRITICAL THINKING PROBLEM 4.2

GENERAL JOURNAL

PAGE ______

DATE		DESCRIPTION	POST. REF.	DEBIT	CREDIT

Name ______________________

CRITICAL THINKING PROBLEM 4.2 (continued)

GENERAL JOURNAL PAGE ______

DATE	DESCRIPTION	POST. REF.	DEBIT	CREDIT

Name ______________________________

CRITICAL THINKING PROBLEM 4.2 (continued)

GENERAL JOURNAL

PAGE ______

	DATE	DESCRIPTION	POST. REF.	DEBIT	CREDIT	
1						1
2						2
3						3
4						4
5						5
6						6
7						7
8						8
9						9
10						10
11						11
12						12
13						13
14						14

GENERAL LEDGER

ACCOUNT ______________________________ ACCOUNT NO. ______

DATE	DESCRIPTION	POST. REF.	DEBIT	CREDIT	BALANCE	
					DEBIT	CREDIT

Name ______________________

CRITICAL THINKING PROBLEM 4.2 (continued)

GENERAL LEDGER

ACCOUNT ______________________ ACCOUNT NO. ________

DATE	DESCRIPTION	POST. REF.	DEBIT	CREDIT	BALANCE DEBIT	BALANCE CREDIT

ACCOUNT ______________________ ACCOUNT NO. ________

DATE	DESCRIPTION	POST. REF.	DEBIT	CREDIT	BALANCE DEBIT	BALANCE CREDIT

ACCOUNT ______________________ ACCOUNT NO. ________

DATE	DESCRIPTION	POST. REF.	DEBIT	CREDIT	BALANCE DEBIT	BALANCE CREDIT

ACCOUNT ______________________ ACCOUNT NO. ________

DATE	DESCRIPTION	POST. REF.	DEBIT	CREDIT	BALANCE DEBIT	BALANCE CREDIT

ACCOUNT ______________________ ACCOUNT NO. ________

DATE	DESCRIPTION	POST. REF.	DEBIT	CREDIT	BALANCE DEBIT	BALANCE CREDIT

Name

CRITICAL THINKING PROBLEM 4.2 (continued)

GENERAL LEDGER

ACCOUNT ______ ACCOUNT NO. ______

DATE		DESCRIPTION	POST. REF.	DEBIT	CREDIT	BALANCE DEBIT	BALANCE CREDIT

ACCOUNT ______ ACCOUNT NO. ______

DATE		DESCRIPTION	POST. REF.	DEBIT	CREDIT	BALANCE DEBIT	BALANCE CREDIT

ACCOUNT ______ ACCOUNT NO. ______

DATE		DESCRIPTION	POST. REF.	DEBIT	CREDIT	BALANCE DEBIT	BALANCE CREDIT

ACCOUNT ______ ACCOUNT NO. ______

DATE		DESCRIPTION	POST. REF.	DEBIT	CREDIT	BALANCE DEBIT	BALANCE CREDIT

ACCOUNT ______ ACCOUNT NO. ______

DATE		DESCRIPTION	POST. REF.	DEBIT	CREDIT	BALANCE DEBIT	BALANCE CREDIT

Name

CRITICAL THINKING PROBLEM 4.2 (continued)

GENERAL LEDGER

ACCOUNT ______ ACCOUNT NO. ______

DATE		DESCRIPTION	POST. REF.	DEBIT	CREDIT	BALANCE DEBIT	BALANCE CREDIT

ACCOUNT ______ ACCOUNT NO. ______

DATE		DESCRIPTION	POST. REF.	DEBIT	CREDIT	BALANCE DEBIT	BALANCE CREDIT

ACCOUNT ______ ACCOUNT NO. ______

DATE		DESCRIPTION	POST. REF.	DEBIT	CREDIT	BALANCE DEBIT	BALANCE CREDIT

EXTRA FORMS

GENERAL LEDGER

ACCOUNT ______ ACCOUNT NO. ______

DATE		DESCRIPTION	POST. REF.	DEBIT	CREDIT	BALANCE DEBIT	BALANCE CREDIT

ACCOUNT ______ ACCOUNT NO. ______

DATE		DESCRIPTION	POST. REF.	DEBIT	CREDIT	BALANCE DEBIT	BALANCE CREDIT

Name

CRITICAL THINKING PROBLEM 4.2 (continued)

ACCOUNT NAME	DEBIT	CREDIT

Name

CRITICAL THINKING PROBLEM 4.2 (continued)

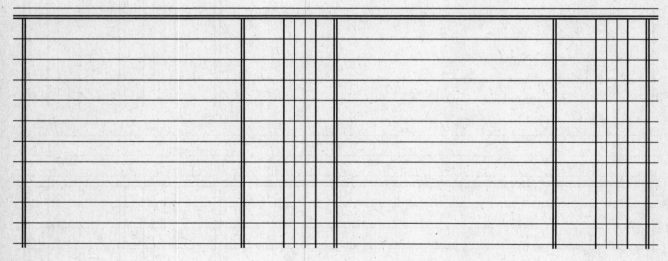

Analyze:

Chapter 4 Practice Test Answer Key

Part A Matching

1. a
2. f
3. b
4. j
5. i
6. h
7. d
8. e
9. c
10. g

Part B Completion

1. ledger
2. posting references
3. brief or concise
4. credit
5. debit
6. debit
7. year
8. chronological or date
9. assets or balance sheet accounts
10. posted

CHAPTER 5

Adjustments and the Worksheet

STUDY GUIDE

STUDY GUIDE

Understanding the Chapter

Objectives

1. Complete a trial balance on a worksheet. **2.** Prepare adjustments for unrecorded business transactions. **3.** Complete the worksheet. **4.** Prepare an income statement, statement of owner's equity, and balance sheet from the completed worksheet. **5.** Journalize and post the adjusting entries. **6.** Define the accounting terms new to this chapter.

Reading Assignment

Read Chapter 5 in the textbook. Complete the textbook Section Self Review as you finish reading each section of the chapter, and the Comprehensive Self Review at the end of the chapter. Refer to the Chapter 5 Glossary or to the Glossary at the end of the book to find definitions for terms that are not familiar to you.

Activities

❑ **Thinking Critically** — Answer the *Thinking Critically* questions for Willamette Valley Vineyards and Managerial Implications.

❑ **Discussion Questions** — Answer each assigned discussion question in Chapter 5.

❑ **Exercises** — Complete each assigned exercise in Chapter 5. Use the forms provided in this SGWP. The objectives covered by an exercise are given after the exercise number. If you need help with an exercise, review the portion of the chapter related to the objective(s) covered.

❑ **Problems A/B** — Complete each assigned problem in Chapter 5. Use the forms provided in this SGWP. The objectives covered by a problem are given after the problem number. If you need help with a problem, review the portion of the chapter related to the objective(s) covered.

❑ **Critical Thinking Problems** — Complete the critical thinking problems as assigned. Use the forms provided in this SGWP.

❑ **Business Connections** — Complete the Business Connections activities as assigned to gain a deeper understanding of Chapter 5 concepts.

Practice Tests

Complete the Practice Tests, which cover the main points in your reading assignment. Compare your answers with those in the Practice Test Answer Key for Chapter 5 at the end of this chapter. If you have answered any questions incorrectly, review the related section of the text.

Part A True-False *For each of the following statements, circle T in the answer column if the statement is true or F if the statement is false.*

(T)	F	**1.** Liability account balances from the trial balance are normally transferred to the Balance Sheet credit column of the worksheet.
T	(F)	**2.** Asset account balances from the trial balance are normally transferred to the Income Statement Debit column of the worksheet.
(T)	F	**3.** The first two money columns of the worksheet contain a trial balance of the general ledger accounts.
(T)	F	**4.** Accountants use a worksheet as a means of organizing their figures quickly.
(T)	F	**5.** The ledger must be in balance before financial statements are prepared.
(T)	F	**6.** The Income Statement columns and Balance Sheet columns provide the figures for preparing the financial statements.
(T)	F	**7.** On a worksheet, the difference between the Debit and Credit Column totals in the Income Statement section must equal the difference between the Debit and Credit column totals in the Balance Sheet section.
(T)	F	**8.** After the net income (or net loss) is computed in the Income Statement section of the worksheet, this amount is transferred to the Balance Sheet section of the worksheet.
T	(F)	**9.** When the Balance Sheet columns of the worksheet are first added, the total of the Debit column should equal the total of the Credit column.
(T)	F	**10.** The balances of the expense accounts are normally transferred to the Income Statement Debit column of the worksheet.

Part B Matching *For each numbered item, choose the matching term from the box and write the identifying letter in the answer column.*

D	**1.** Assets = Liabilities + Owner's Equity.
B	**2.** A way to test the accuracy of the figures recorded in the general ledger.
C	**3.** The term used for an account with an excess of debits over credits.
F	**4.** The term used when the total of the debit amounts in the general ledger and the total of the credit amounts are equal.
E	**5.** The term used when referring to an account in which there is an excess of credits over debits.
A	**6.** A form used to organize the amounts needed to prepare the financial statements.

a. Worksheet
b. Trial balance
c. Debit balance
d. Fundamental accounting equation
e. Credit balance
f. In balance

Demonstration Problem

The general ledger accounts listed on the worksheet for the Atwell Graphics Design Company on January 31, 2016, show the results of the first month of operation.

Instructions

1. Record the following adjustments in the Adjustments section of the worksheet using the information below.
   - **a.** Supplies used during the month, $4,425.
   - **b.** The amount in the **Prepaid Rent** account represents a payment made on January 1 for the rent for 12 months.
   - **c.** The equipment, purchased in January, has an estimated useful life of 10 years with no salvage value. The firm uses the straight-line method of depreciation.
2. Complete the worksheet.
3. Journalize and post the adjusting entries. Use journal page number 2. Use account numbers from accounts in working papers in General Ledger.

SOLUTION

Atwell Graphics Design Company

Worksheet

Month Ended January 31, 2016

ACCOUNT NAME	TRIAL BALANCE		ADJUSTMENTS		ADJUSTED TRIAL BALANCE		INCOME STATEMENT		BALANCE SHEET	
	DEBIT	CREDIT	DEBIT	CREDIT	DEBIT	CREDIT	DEBIT	CREDIT	DEBIT	CREDIT
Cash	37,350.00				37,350.00				37,350.00	
Accounts Receivable	50,700.00				50,700.00				50,700.00	
Supplies	8,700.00			(a) 4,425.00	4,275.00				4,275.00	
Prepaid Rent	126,000.00			(b)10,500.00	115,500.00				115,500.00	
Equipment	126,000.00				126,000.00				126,000.00	
Accum. Depr.—Equipment				(c) 1,050.00		1,050.00				1,050.00
Accounts Payable		80,400.00				80,400.00				80,400.00
John Atwell, Capital		147,600.00				147,600.00				147,600.00
John Atwell, Drawing	9,000.00				9,000.00				9,000.00	
Fees Income		226,515.00				226,515.00		226,515.00		
Advertising Expense	11,400.00				11,400.00		11,400.00			
Insurance Expense	12,000.00				12,000.00		12,000.00			
Salaries Expense	67,500.00				67,500.00		67,500.00			
Supplies Expense			(a) 4,425.00		4,425.00		4,425.00			
Rent Expense			(b)10,500.00		10,500.00		10,500.00			
Telephone Expense	2,625.00				2,625.00		2,625.00			
Utilities Expense	3,240.00				3,240.00		3,240.00			
Depr. Expense—Equipment			(c) 1,050.00		1,050.00		1,050.00			
Totals	454,515.00	454,515.00	15,975.00	15,975.00	455,565.00	455,565.00	112,740.00	226,515.00	342,825.00	229,050.00
Net Income							113,775.00			113,775.00
							226,515.00	226,515.00	342,825.00	342,825.00

SOLUTION (continued)

GENERAL JOURNAL

PAGE 2

DATE		DESCRIPTION	POST. REF.	DEBIT	CREDIT
		Adjusting Entries			
2016					
Jan.	31	Supplies Expense	518	4425 00	
		Supplies	121		4425 00
	31	Rent Expense	519	10500 00	
		Prepaid Rent	131		10500 00
	31	Depreciation Expense—Equipment	524	1050 00	
		Accumulated Depreciation—Equipment	142		1050 00

GENERAL LEDGER (PARTIAL)

ACCOUNT **Supplies** ACCOUNT NO. **121**

DATE		DESCRIPTION	POST. REF.	DEBIT	CREDIT	BALANCE DEBIT	BALANCE CREDIT
2016							
Jan.	3		J1	8700 00		8700 00	
	31	Adjusting	J2		4425 00	4275 00	

ACCOUNT **Prepaid Rent** ACCOUNT NO. **131**

DATE		DESCRIPTION	POST. REF.	DEBIT	CREDIT	BALANCE DEBIT	BALANCE CREDIT
2016							
Jan.	2		J1	126000 00		126000 00	
	31	Adjusting	J2		10500 00	115500 00	

ACCOUNT **Accumulated Depreciation—Equipment** ACCOUNT NO. **142**

DATE		DESCRIPTION	POST. REF.	DEBIT	CREDIT	BALANCE DEBIT	BALANCE CREDIT
2016							
Jan.	31	Adjusting	J2		1050 00		1050 00

SOLUTION (continued)

GENERAL LEDGER (PARTIAL)

ACCOUNT **Supplies Expense** ACCOUNT NO. **518**

DATE		DESCRIPTION	POST. REF.	DEBIT	CREDIT	BALANCE DEBIT	BALANCE CREDIT
2016							
Jan.	**31**	**Adjusting**	**J2**	**4 4 2 5 00**		**4 4 2 5 00**	

ACCOUNT **Rent Expense** ACCOUNT NO. **519**

DATE		DESCRIPTION	POST. REF.	DEBIT	CREDIT	BALANCE DEBIT	BALANCE CREDIT
2016							
Jan.	**31**	**Adjusting**	**J2**	**10 5 0 0 00**		**10 5 0 0 00**	

ACCOUNT **Depreciation Expense—Equipment** ACCOUNT NO. **524**

DATE		DESCRIPTION	POST. REF.	DEBIT	CREDIT	BALANCE DEBIT	BALANCE CREDIT
2016							
Jan.	**31**	**Adjusting**	**J2**	**1 0 5 0 00**		**1 0 5 0 00**	

WORKING PAPERS

Name ______________________________

EXERCISE 5.1

1. ______________________________

2. ______________________________

3. ______________________________

EXERCISE 5.2

1. ______________________________

2. ______________________________

Name

EXERCISE 5.3

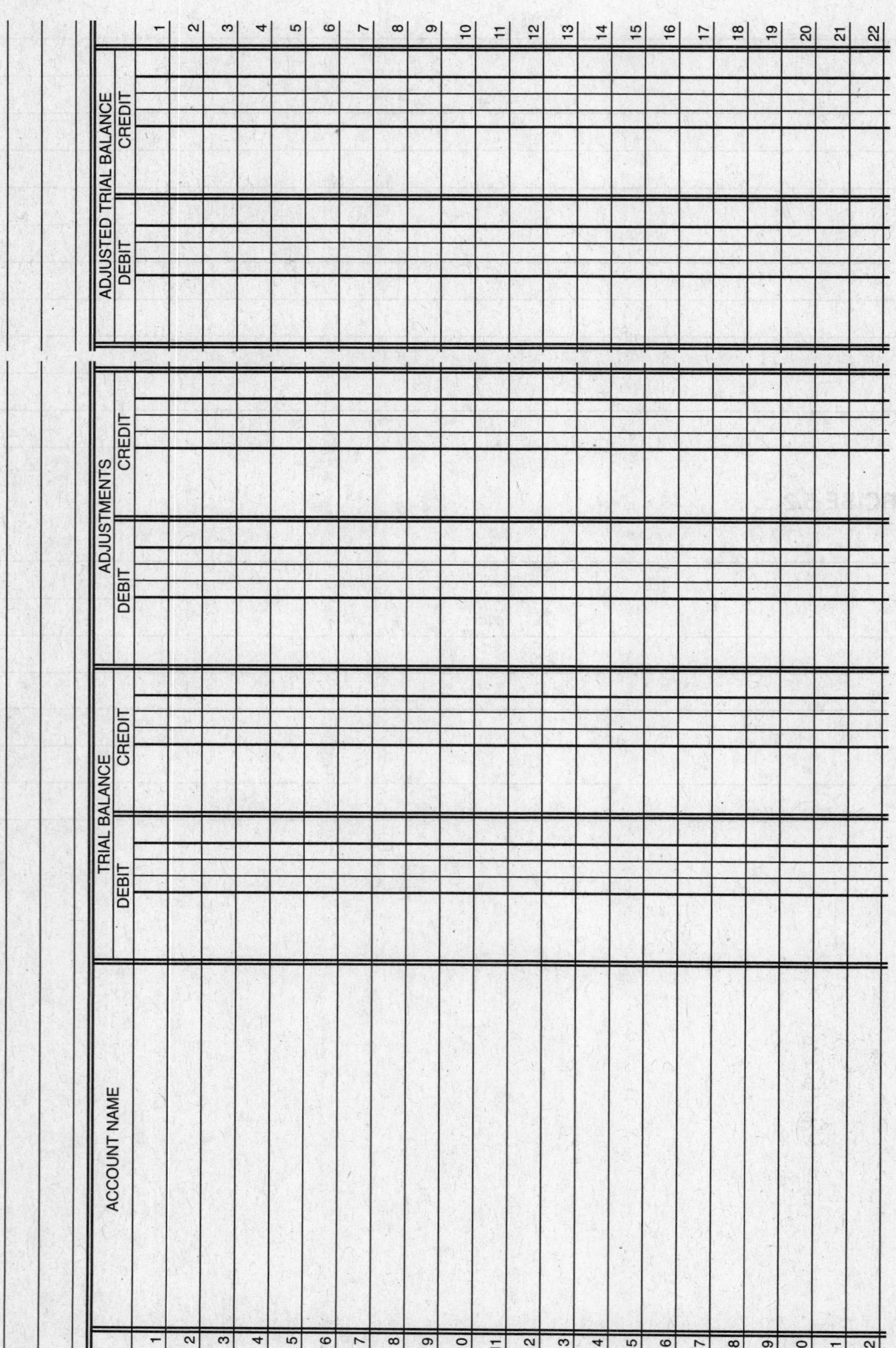

Name

EXERCISE 5.4

Name

EXERCISE 5.5

GENERAL JOURNAL

PAGE

	DATE		DESCRIPTION	POST. REF.	DEBIT	CREDIT	
1							1
2							2
3							3
4							4
5							5
6							6
7							7
8							8
9							9
10							10
11							11

GENERAL LEDGER

ACCOUNT **Supplies** ACCOUNT NO. **121**

DATE		DESCRIPTION	POST. REF.	DEBIT	CREDIT	BALANCE	
						DEBIT	CREDIT

ACCOUNT **Prepaid Insurance** ACCOUNT NO. **131**

DATE		DESCRIPTION	POST. REF.	DEBIT	CREDIT	BALANCE	
						DEBIT	CREDIT

ACCOUNT **Accumulated Depreciation—Equipment** ACCOUNT NO. **142**

DATE		DESCRIPTION	POST. REF.	DEBIT	CREDIT	BALANCE	
						DEBIT	CREDIT

Name

EXERCISE 5.5 (continued)

GENERAL LEDGER

ACCOUNT **Depreciation Expense—Equipment** ACCOUNT NO. **517**

DATE		DESCRIPTION	POST. REF.	DEBIT	CREDIT	BALANCE	
						DEBIT	CREDIT

ACCOUNT **Insurance Expense** ACCOUNT NO. **521**

DATE		DESCRIPTION	POST. REF.	DEBIT	CREDIT	BALANCE	
						DEBIT	CREDIT

ACCOUNT **Supplies Expense** ACCOUNT NO. **523**

DATE		DESCRIPTION	POST. REF.	DEBIT	CREDIT	BALANCE	
						DEBIT	CREDIT

EXTRA FORMS

ACCOUNT ACCOUNT NO.

DATE		DESCRIPTION	POST. REF.	DEBIT	CREDIT	BALANCE	
						DEBIT	CREDIT

ACCOUNT ACCOUNT NO.

DATE		DESCRIPTION	POST. REF.	DEBIT	CREDIT	BALANCE	
						DEBIT	CREDIT

Name

PROBLEM 5.1A or 5.1B

	ACCOUNT NAME	TRIAL BALANCE		ADJUSTMENTS	
		DEBIT	CREDIT	DEBIT	CREDIT
1					
2					
3					
4					
5					
6					
7					
8					
9					
10					
11					
12					
13					
14					
15					
16					
17					
18					
19					
20					
21					
22					
23					
24					
25					
26					
27					
28					
29					
30					
31					
32					

Name

PROBLEM 5.1A or 5.1B (continued)

ADJUSTED TRIAL BALANCE		INCOME STATEMENT		BALANCE SHEET		
DEBIT	CREDIT	DEBIT	CREDIT	DEBIT	CREDIT	
						1
						2
						3
						4
						5
						6
						7
						8
						9
						10
						11
						12
						13
						14
						15
						16
						17
						18
						19
						20
						21
						22
						23
						24
						25
						26
						27
						28
						29
						30
						31
						32

Analyze:

Name ______________________

PROBLEM 5.2A or 5.2B

	ACCOUNT NAME	TRIAL BALANCE		ADJUSTMENTS	
		DEBIT	CREDIT	DEBIT	CREDIT
1					
2					
3					
4					
5					
6					
7					
8					
9					
10					
11					
12					
13					
14					
15					
16					
17					
18					
19					
20					
21					
22					
23					
24					
25					
26					
27					
28					
29					
30					
31					
32					

Name ______________________________

PROBLEM 5.2A or 5.2B (continued)

ADJUSTED TRIAL BALANCE		INCOME STATEMENT		BALANCE SHEET	
DEBIT	CREDIT	DEBIT	CREDIT	DEBIT	CREDIT

Analyze: ______________________________

Name

PROBLEM 5.3A or 5.3B

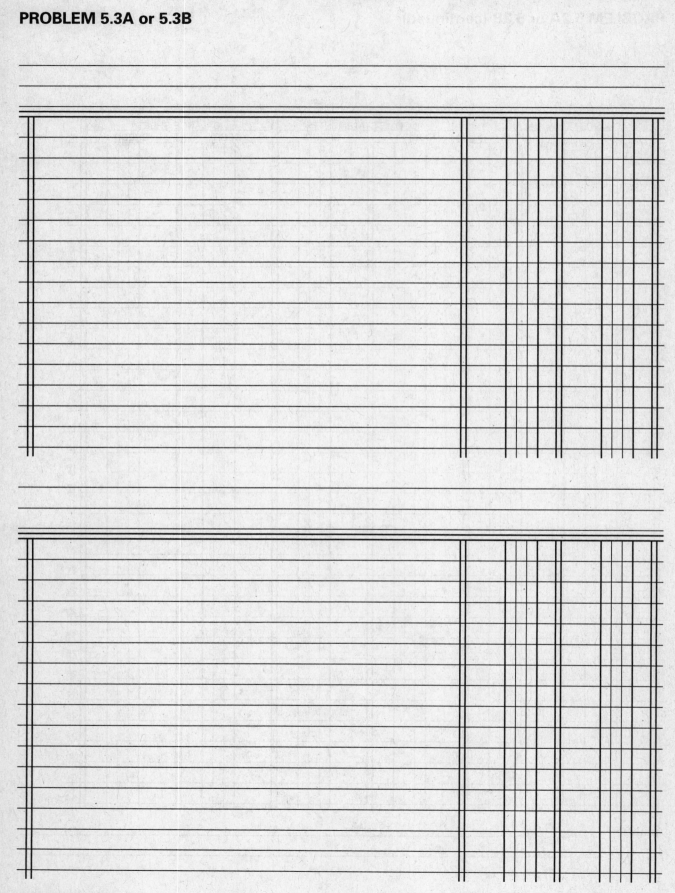

Name

PROBLEM 5.3A or 5.3B (continued)

Analyze:

Name

PROBLEM 5.4A or 5.4B

ACCOUNT NAME	TRIAL BALANCE		ADJUSTMENTS	
	DEBIT	CREDIT	DEBIT	CREDIT

Name ______________________

PROBLEM 5.4A or 5.4B (continued)

ADJUSTED TRIAL BALANCE		INCOME STATEMENT		BALANCE SHEET		
DEBIT	CREDIT	DEBIT	CREDIT	DEBIT	CREDIT	
						1
						2
						3
						4
						5
						6
						7
						8
						9
						10
						11
						12
						13
						14
						15
						16
						17
						18
						19
						20
						21
						22
						23
						24
						25
						26
						27
						28
						29
						30
						31
						32

Name

PROBLEM 5.4A or 5.4B (continued)

Name

PROBLEM 5.4A or 5.4B (continued)

Name

PROBLEM 5.4A or 5.4B (continued)

GENERAL JOURNAL

PAGE

DATE		DESCRIPTION	POST. REF.	DEBIT	CREDIT

GENERAL LEDGER

ACCOUNT ACCOUNT NO.

DATE		DESCRIPTION	POST. REF.	DEBIT	CREDIT	BALANCE	
						DEBIT	CREDIT

ACCOUNT ACCOUNT NO.

DATE		DESCRIPTION	POST. REF.	DEBIT	CREDIT	BALANCE	
						DEBIT	CREDIT

ACCOUNT ACCOUNT NO.

DATE		DESCRIPTION	POST. REF.	DEBIT	CREDIT	BALANCE	
						DEBIT	CREDIT

Name

PROBLEM 5.4A or 5.4B (continued)

GENERAL LEDGER

ACCOUNT ______ ACCOUNT NO. ______

DATE		DESCRIPTION	POST. REF.	DEBIT	CREDIT	BALANCE DEBIT	BALANCE CREDIT

ACCOUNT ______ ACCOUNT NO. ______

DATE		DESCRIPTION	POST. REF.	DEBIT	CREDIT	BALANCE DEBIT	BALANCE CREDIT

ACCOUNT ______ ACCOUNT NO. ______

DATE		DESCRIPTION	POST. REF.	DEBIT	CREDIT	BALANCE DEBIT	BALANCE CREDIT

ACCOUNT ______ ACCOUNT NO. ______

DATE		DESCRIPTION	POST. REF.	DEBIT	CREDIT	BALANCE DEBIT	BALANCE CREDIT

ACCOUNT ______ ACCOUNT NO. ______

DATE		DESCRIPTION	POST. REF.	DEBIT	CREDIT	BALANCE DEBIT	BALANCE CREDIT

Analyze: ______

Name ______________________

CRITICAL THINKING PROBLEM 5.1

	ACCOUNT NAME	TRIAL BALANCE		ADJUSTMENTS	
		DEBIT	CREDIT	DEBIT	CREDIT
1					
2					
3					
4					
5					
6					
7					
8					
9					
10					
11					
12					
13					
14					
15					
16					
17					
18					
19					
20					
21					
22					
23					
24					
25					
26					
27					
28					
29					
30					
31					
32					

Name ______________________________

CRITICAL THINKING PROBLEM 5.1 (continued)

ADJUSTED TRIAL BALANCE		INCOME STATEMENT		BALANCE SHEET		
DEBIT	CREDIT	DEBIT	CREDIT	DEBIT	CREDIT	
						1
						2
						3
						4
						5
						6
						7
						8
						9
						10
						11
						12
						13
						14
						15
						16
						17
						18
						19
						20
						21
						22
						23
						24
						25
						26
						27
						28
						29
						30
						31
						32

Name

CRITICAL THINKING PROBLEM 5.1 (continued)

Name

CRITICAL THINKING PROBLEM 5.1 (continued)

Name ______________________________

CRITICAL THINKING PROBLEM 5.1 (continued)

GENERAL JOURNAL PAGE ______

	DATE	DESCRIPTION	POST. REF.	DEBIT	CREDIT	
1						1
2						2
3						3
4						4
5						5
6						6
7						7
8						8
9						9
10						10
11						11

GENERAL LEDGER

ACCOUNT ______________________ ACCOUNT NO. ______

DATE	DESCRIPTION	POST. REF.	DEBIT	CREDIT	BALANCE	
					DEBIT	CREDIT

ACCOUNT ______________________ ACCOUNT NO. ______

DATE	DESCRIPTION	POST. REF.	DEBIT	CREDIT	BALANCE	
					DEBIT	CREDIT

ACCOUNT ______________________ ACCOUNT NO. ______

DATE	DESCRIPTION	POST. REF.	DEBIT	CREDIT	BALANCE	
					DEBIT	CREDIT

Name

CRITICAL THINKING PROBLEM 5.1 (continued)

GENERAL LEDGER

ACCOUNT ______ ACCOUNT NO. ______

DATE		DESCRIPTION	POST. REF.	DEBIT	CREDIT	BALANCE DEBIT	BALANCE CREDIT

ACCOUNT ______ ACCOUNT NO. ______

DATE		DESCRIPTION	POST. REF.	DEBIT	CREDIT	BALANCE DEBIT	BALANCE CREDIT

ACCOUNT ______ ACCOUNT NO. ______

DATE		DESCRIPTION	POST. REF.	DEBIT	CREDIT	BALANCE DEBIT	BALANCE CREDIT

Analyze: ______

EXTRA FORMS

ACCOUNT ______ ACCOUNT NO. ______

DATE		DESCRIPTION	POST. REF.	DEBIT	CREDIT	BALANCE DEBIT	BALANCE CREDIT

ACCOUNT ______ ACCOUNT NO. ______

DATE		DESCRIPTION	POST. REF.	DEBIT	CREDIT	BALANCE DEBIT	BALANCE CREDIT

Name

CRITICAL THINKING PROBLEM 5.2

TO:

FROM:

DATE:

SUBJECT:

Chapter 5 Practice Test Answer Key

Part A True-False

1. T	**6. T**
2. F	**7. T**
3. T	**8. T**
4. T	**9. F**
5. T	**10. T**

Part B Matching

1. d	**4. f**
2. b	**5. e**
3. c	**6. a**

CHAPTER 6

Closing Entries and the Postclosing Trial Balance

STUDY GUIDE

Understanding the Chapter

Objectives

1. Journalize and post closing entries. **2.** Prepare a postclosing trial balance. **3.** Interpret financial statements. **4.** Review the steps in the accounting cycle. **5.** Define the accouning terms new to this chapter.

Reading Assignment

Read Chapter 6 in the textbook. Complete the textbook Section Self Review as you finish reading each section of the chapter, and the Comprehensive Self Review at the end of the chapter. Refer to the Chapter 6 Glossary or to the Glossary at the end of the book to find definitions for terms that are not familiar to you.

Activities

❑ **Thinking Critically** — Answer the *Thinking Critically* questions for Carnival Corporation and Managerial Implications.

❑ **Discussion Questions** — Answer each assigned discussion question in Chapter 6.

❑ **Exercises** — Complete each assigned exercise in Chapter 6. Use the forms provided in this SGWP. The objectives covered by an exercise are given after the exercise number. If you need help with an exercise, review the portion of the chapter related to the objective(s) covered.

❑ **Problems A/B** — Complete each assigned problem in Chapter 6. Use the forms provided in this SGWP. The objectives covered by a problem are given after the problem number. If you need help with a problem, review the portion of the chapter related to the objective(s) covered.

❑ **Critical Thinking Problems** — Complete the critical thinking problems as assigned. Use the forms provided in this SGWP.

❑ **Business Connections** — Complete the Business Connections activities as assigned to gain a deeper understanding of Chapter 6 concepts.

Practice Tests

Complete the Practice Tests, which cover the main points in your reading assignment. Compare your answers with those in the Practice Test Answer Key for Chapter 6 at the end of this chapter. If you have answered any questions incorrectly, review the related section of the text.

STUDY GUIDE

Part A True-False *For each of the following statements, circle T in the answer column if the statement is true or F if the statement is false.*

T F **1.** All asset accounts are closed into the **Income Summary** account.

T F **2.** The balance of the **Income Summary** account—net income or net loss—is transferred to the owner's capital account.

T F **3.** The Income Summary is a financial statement prepared at the end of each accounting period.

T F **4.** Adjusting entries create a permanent record of any changes in account balances that are shown on the worksheet.

T F **5.** If an adjustment is not made for supplies used, the net income for the period will be understated.

T F **6.** Closing entries reduce the balance of revenue and asset accounts to zero so that they are ready to receive data for the next period.

T F **7.** The general ledger is a continuing record.

T F **8.** The postclosing trial balance will show figures for asset, liability, owner's equity, revenue, and expense accounts.

T F **9.** The total of all expenses appears on the credit side of the **Income Summary** account.

T F **10.** To close a revenue account, the accountant debits that account and credits the **Income Summary** account.

Part B Matching *For each numbered item, choose the matching term from the box and write the identifying letter in the answer column.*

a. Closing the accounting records
b. Closing entries
c. Closed account
d. Postclosing trial balance
e. Income Summary

____ **1.** The last step in the end-of-period procedure, which shows the accountant that it is safe to proceed with entries for the new period.

____ **2.** Term used when referring to an account after its balance has been transferred out.

____ **3.** Special account in the general ledger used for combining data about revenue and expenses.

____ **4.** Journal entries used to transfer the balances of the revenue and expense accounts to the income summary account as part of the end-of-period procedures.

____ **5.** The procedure of journalizing and posting the results of operations at the end of an accounting period.

Demonstration Problem

The Income Statement and Balance Sheet sections of the worksheet for Alexander Thomas for the period ended December 31, 2016 are shown below.

Instructions

1. Journalize the closing entries on page 24 of a general journal.
2. Determine the new balance for Capital once the closing entries have been posted.

Alexander Thomas

Worksheet

Month Ended December 31, 2016

	ACCOUNT NAME	INCOME STATEMENT		BALANCE SHEET	
		DEBIT	CREDIT	DEBIT	CREDIT
1	**Cash**			48,000.00	
2	**Accounts Receivable**			3,000.00	
3	**Supplies**			6,000.00	
4	**Prepaid Rent**			4,500.00	
5	**Equipment**			30,000.00	
6	**Accumulated Depreciation—Equipment**				720.00
7	**Accounts Payable**				7,500.00
8	**Alexander Thomas, Capital**				54,750.00
9	**Alexander Thomas, Drawing**			3,000.00	
10	**Fees Income**		45,000.00		
11	**Salaries Expense**	7,200.00			
12	**Utilities Expense**	1,050.00			
13	**Supplies Expense**	2,400.00			
14	**Advertising Expense**	2,100.00			
15	**Depreciation Expense—Equipment**	720.00			
16	**Totals**	13,470.00	45,000.00	94,500.00	62,970.00
17	**Net Income**	31,530.00			31,530.00
18		45,000.00	45,000.00	94,500.00	94,500.00
19					

SOLUTION

GENERAL JOURNAL

PAGE 24

DATE		DESCRIPTION	POST. REF.	DEBIT	CREDIT
		Closing Entries			
2016					
Dec.	**31**	**Fees Income**		**45000 00**	
		Income Summary			**45000 00**
	31	**Income Summary**		**13470 00**	
		Salaries Expense			**7200 00**
		Utilities Expense			**1050 00**
		Supplies Expense			**2400 00**
		Advertising Expense			**2100 00**
		Depreciation Expense—Equipment			**720 00**
	31	**Income Summary**		**31530 00**	
		Alexander Thomas, Capital			**31530 00**
	31	**Alexander Thomas, Capital**		**3000 00**	
		Alexander Thomas, Drawing			**3000 00**

New Capital Balance:		
Alexander Thomas, Capital, December 1, 2016		**$54,750.00**
Add: Net Income	**31,530.00**	
Less Withdrawals for December	**3,000.00**	
Increase in Capital		**28,530.00**
Alexander Thomas, Capital, December 31, 2016		**$83,280.00**

WORKING PAPERS

Name ____________________

EXERCISE 6.1

GENERAL JOURNAL PAGE ______

	DATE		DESCRIPTION	POST. REF.	DEBIT	CREDIT	
1							1
2							2
3							3
4							4
5							5
6							6
7							7
8							8
9							9
10							10
11							11
12							12
13							13
14							14
15							15
16							16
17							17
18							18
19							19
20							20
21							21

EXERCISE 6.2

1. ____________________

2. ____________________

3. ____________________

4. ____________________

5. ____________________

6. ____________________

7. ____________________

8. ____________________

9. ____________________

Name ______________________________

EXERCISE 6.3

1. ______________________________
2. ______________________________
3. ______________________________
4. ______________________________
5. ______________________________
6. ______________________________
7. ______________________________

EXERCISE 6.4

1. ____________________
2. ____________________
3. ____________________
4. ____________________
5. ____________________
6. ____________________
7. ____________________
8. ____________________
9. ____________________
10. ____________________
11. ____________________
12. ____________________
13. ____________________
14. ____________________
15. ____________________

EXERCISE 6.5

1. Total revenue for the period is __________.

2. Total expenses for the period are __________.

3. Net income for the period is __________.

4. Owner's withdrawals for the period are __________.

Name

EXERCISE 6.6

GENERAL JOURNAL

PAGE

DATE		DESCRIPTION	POST. REF.	DEBIT	CREDIT

Name

EXERCISE 6.6 (continued)

GENERAL LEDGER

ACCOUNT Lee Retha Hale, Capital — ACCOUNT NO. 301

DATE		DESCRIPTION	POST. REF.	DEBIT	CREDIT	BALANCE DEBIT	BALANCE CREDIT
2016							
Mar.	31	Balance	✔				80 0 0 0 00

ACCOUNT Lee Retha Hale, Drawing — ACCOUNT NO. 302

DATE		DESCRIPTION	POST. REF.	DEBIT	CREDIT	BALANCE DEBIT	BALANCE CREDIT
2016							
Mar.	31	Balance	✔			13 0 0 0 00	

ACCOUNT Income Summary — ACCOUNT NO. 399

DATE		DESCRIPTION	POST. REF.	DEBIT	CREDIT	BALANCE DEBIT	BALANCE CREDIT

ACCOUNT Fees Income — ACCOUNT NO. 401

DATE		DESCRIPTION	POST. REF.	DEBIT	CREDIT	BALANCE DEBIT	BALANCE CREDIT
2016							
Mar.	31	Balance	✔				374 4 6 0 00

ACCOUNT Depreciation Expense—Equipment — ACCOUNT NO. 510

DATE		DESCRIPTION	POST. REF.	DEBIT	CREDIT	BALANCE DEBIT	BALANCE CREDIT
2016							
Mar.	31	Balance	✔			21 1 6 0 00	

Name

EXERCISE 6.6 (continued)

GENERAL LEDGER

ACCOUNT Insurance Expense ACCOUNT NO. 511

DATE		DESCRIPTION	POST. REF.	DEBIT	CREDIT	BALANCE DEBIT	BALANCE CREDIT
2016							
Mar.	31	Balance	✔			11 4 0 0 00	

ACCOUNT Rent Expense ACCOUNT NO. 514

DATE		DESCRIPTION	POST. REF.	DEBIT	CREDIT	BALANCE DEBIT	BALANCE CREDIT
2016							
Mar.	31	Balance	✔			33 0 0 0 00	

ACCOUNT Salaries Expense ACCOUNT NO. 517

DATE		DESCRIPTION	POST. REF.	DEBIT	CREDIT	BALANCE DEBIT	BALANCE CREDIT
2016							
Mar.	31	Balance	✔			166 0 0 0 00	

ACCOUNT Supplies Expense ACCOUNT NO. 518

DATE		DESCRIPTION	POST. REF.	DEBIT	CREDIT	BALANCE DEBIT	BALANCE CREDIT
2016							
Mar.	31	Balance	✔			5 6 0 0 00	

ACCOUNT Telephone Expense ACCOUNT NO. 519

DATE		DESCRIPTION	POST. REF.	DEBIT	CREDIT	BALANCE DEBIT	BALANCE CREDIT
2016							
Mar.	31	Balance	✔			6 8 0 0 00	

Name

EXERCISE 6.6 (continued)

GENERAL LEDGER

ACCOUNT **Utilities Expense** ACCOUNT NO. **523**

DATE		DESCRIPTION	POST. REF.	DEBIT	CREDIT	BALANCE DEBIT	BALANCE CREDIT
2016							
Mar.	**31**	**Balance**	**✔**			**9 4 0 0 00**	

EXTRA FORMS

ACCOUNT ACCOUNT NO.

DATE		DESCRIPTION	POST. REF.	DEBIT	CREDIT	BALANCE DEBIT	BALANCE CREDIT

ACCOUNT ACCOUNT NO.

DATE		DESCRIPTION	POST. REF.	DEBIT	CREDIT	BALANCE DEBIT	BALANCE CREDIT

ACCOUNT ACCOUNT NO.

DATE		DESCRIPTION	POST. REF.	DEBIT	CREDIT	BALANCE DEBIT	BALANCE CREDIT

Name

EXERCISE 6.7

GENERAL JOURNAL

PAGE

	DATE		DESCRIPTION	POST. REF.	DEBIT	CREDIT	
1							1
2							2
3							3
4							4
5							5
6							6
7							7
8							8

EXERCISE 6.8

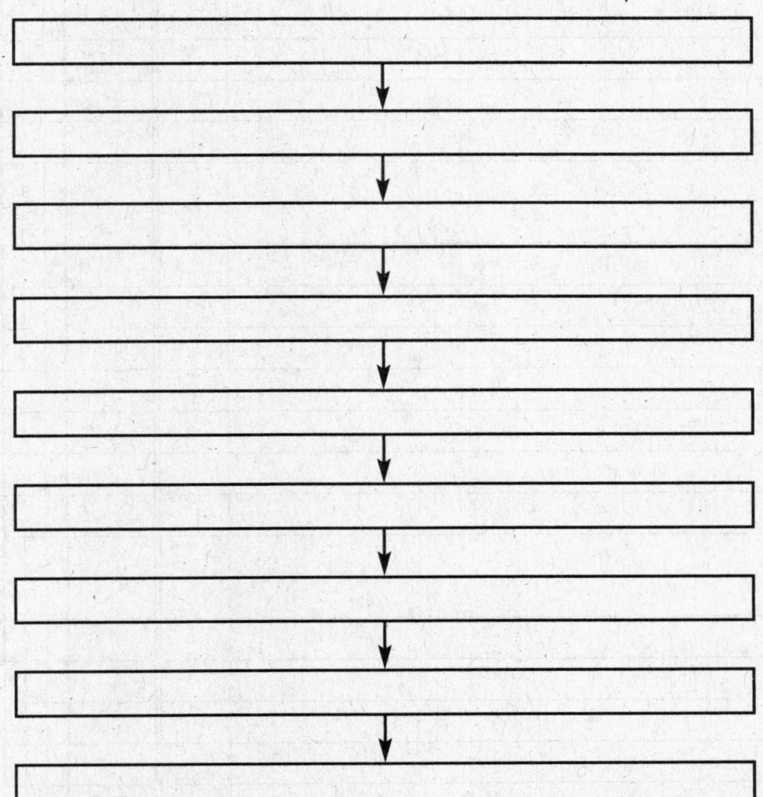

Name

PROBLEM 6.1A or 6.1B

GENERAL JOURNAL

PAGE

DATE		DESCRIPTION	POST. REF.	DEBIT	CREDIT

GENERAL JOURNAL

PAGE

DATE		DESCRIPTION	POST. REF.	DEBIT	CREDIT

Analyze:

Name ____________________

PROBLEM 6.2A or 6.2B

GENERAL JOURNAL

PAGE ____

	DATE		DESCRIPTION	POST. REF.	DEBIT	CREDIT	
1							1
2							2
3							3
4							4
5							5
6							6
7							7
8							8
9							9
10							10
11							11

GENERAL JOURNAL

PAGE ____

	DATE		DESCRIPTION	POST. REF.	DEBIT	CREDIT	
1							1
2							2
3							3
4							4
5							5
6							6
7							7
8							8
9							9
10							10
11							11
12							12
13							13
14							14
15							15
16							16
17							17
18							18

Name

PROBLEM 6.2A or 6.2B (continued)

GENERAL LEDGER

ACCOUNT **Supplies** ACCOUNT NO. **121**

DATE		DESCRIPTION	POST. REF.	DEBIT	CREDIT	BALANCE DEBIT	BALANCE CREDIT

ACCOUNT **Prepaid Advertising** ACCOUNT NO. **131**

DATE		DESCRIPTION	POST. REF.	DEBIT	CREDIT	BALANCE DEBIT	BALANCE CREDIT

ACCOUNT **Accumulated Depreciation—Equipment** ACCOUNT NO. **142**

DATE		DESCRIPTION	POST. REF.	DEBIT	CREDIT	BALANCE DEBIT	BALANCE CREDIT

ACCOUNT **Capital** ACCOUNT NO. **301**

DATE		DESCRIPTION	POST. REF.	DEBIT	CREDIT	BALANCE DEBIT	BALANCE CREDIT

ACCOUNT **Drawing** ACCOUNT NO. **302**

DATE		DESCRIPTION	POST. REF.	DEBIT	CREDIT	BALANCE DEBIT	BALANCE CREDIT

Name

PROBLEM 6.2A or 6.2B (continued)

GENERAL LEDGER

ACCOUNT **Income Summary** ACCOUNT NO. **399**

DATE		DESCRIPTION	POST. REF.	DEBIT	CREDIT	BALANCE DEBIT	BALANCE CREDIT

ACCOUNT **Fees Income** ACCOUNT NO. **401**

DATE		DESCRIPTION	POST. REF.	DEBIT	CREDIT	BALANCE DEBIT	BALANCE CREDIT

GENERAL LEDGER

ACCOUNT **Salaries Expense** ACCOUNT NO. **511**

DATE		DESCRIPTION	POST. REF.	DEBIT	CREDIT	BALANCE DEBIT	BALANCE CREDIT

ACCOUNT **Utilities Expense** ACCOUNT NO. **514**

DATE		DESCRIPTION	POST. REF.	DEBIT	CREDIT	BALANCE DEBIT	BALANCE CREDIT

ACCOUNT **Supplies Expense** ACCOUNT NO. **517**

DATE		DESCRIPTION	POST. REF.	DEBIT	CREDIT	BALANCE DEBIT	BALANCE CREDIT

Name

PROBLEM 6.2A or 6.2B (continued)

ACCOUNT **Depreciation Expense—Equipment** ACCOUNT NO. **523**

DATE	DESCRIPTION	POST. REF.	DEBIT	CREDIT	BALANCE DEBIT	BALANCE CREDIT

ACCOUNT **Advertising Expense** ACCOUNT NO. **526**

DATE	DESCRIPTION	POST. REF.	DEBIT	CREDIT	BALANCE DEBIT	BALANCE CREDIT

ACCOUNT NAME	DEBIT	CREDIT

Analyze:

Name ______________________

PROBLEM 6.3A or 6.3B

GENERAL JOURNAL

PAGE ______

DATE		DESCRIPTION	POST. REF.	DEBIT	CREDIT

Name

PROBLEM 6.3A or 6.3B (continued)

GENERAL LEDGER

ACCOUNT **Capital** ACCOUNT NO. **301**

DATE		DESCRIPTION	POST. REF.	DEBIT	CREDIT	BALANCE DEBIT	BALANCE CREDIT

ACCOUNT **Drawing** ACCOUNT NO. **302**

DATE		DESCRIPTION	POST. REF.	DEBIT	CREDIT	BALANCE DEBIT	BALANCE CREDIT

ACCOUNT **Income Summary** ACCOUNT NO. **399**

DATE		DESCRIPTION	POST. REF.	DEBIT	CREDIT	BALANCE DEBIT	BALANCE CREDIT

ACCOUNT **Fees Income** ACCOUNT NO. **401**

DATE		DESCRIPTION	POST. REF.	DEBIT	CREDIT	BALANCE DEBIT	BALANCE CREDIT

Name

PROBLEM 6.3A or 6.3B (continued)

GENERAL LEDGER

ACCOUNT **Advertising Expense** ACCOUNT NO. **511**

DATE	DESCRIPTION	POST. REF.	DEBIT	CREDIT	BALANCE DEBIT	BALANCE CREDIT

ACCOUNT **Depreciation Expense—Equipment** ACCOUNT NO. **514**

DATE	DESCRIPTION	POST. REF.	DEBIT	CREDIT	BALANCE DEBIT	BALANCE CREDIT

ACCOUNT **Rent Expense** ACCOUNT NO. **517**

DATE	DESCRIPTION	POST. REF.	DEBIT	CREDIT	BALANCE DEBIT	BALANCE CREDIT

ACCOUNT **Salaries Expense** ACCOUNT NO. **519**

DATE	DESCRIPTION	POST. REF.	DEBIT	CREDIT	BALANCE DEBIT	BALANCE CREDIT

ACCOUNT **Utilities Expense** ACCOUNT NO. **523**

DATE	DESCRIPTION	POST. REF.	DEBIT	CREDIT	BALANCE DEBIT	BALANCE CREDIT

Analyze:

Name

PROBLEM 6.3A or 6.3B (continued)

GENERAL LEDGER

ACCOUNT ACCOUNT NO.

DATE	DESCRIPTION	POST. REF.	DEBIT	CREDIT	BALANCE	
					DEBIT	CREDIT

ACCOUNT ACCOUNT NO.

DATE	DESCRIPTION	POST. REF.	DEBIT	CREDIT	BALANCE	
					DEBIT	CREDIT

ACCOUNT ACCOUNT NO.

DATE	DESCRIPTION	POST. REF.	DEBIT	CREDIT	BALANCE	
					DEBIT	CREDIT

ACCOUNT ACCOUNT NO.

DATE	DESCRIPTION	POST. REF.	DEBIT	CREDIT	BALANCE	
					DEBIT	CREDIT

ACCOUNT ACCOUNT NO.

DATE	DESCRIPTION	POST. REF.	DEBIT	CREDIT	BALANCE	
					DEBIT	CREDIT

Name ______________________________

PROBLEM 6.3A or 6.3B (continued)

GENERAL LEDGER

ACCOUNT ______________________________ ACCOUNT NO. __________

DATE	DESCRIPTION	POST. REF.	DEBIT	CREDIT	BALANCE	
					DEBIT	CREDIT

ACCOUNT ______________________________ ACCOUNT NO. __________

DATE	DESCRIPTION	POST. REF.	DEBIT	CREDIT	BALANCE	
					DEBIT	CREDIT

ACCOUNT ______________________________ ACCOUNT NO. __________

DATE	DESCRIPTION	POST. REF.	DEBIT	CREDIT	BALANCE	
					DEBIT	CREDIT

ACCOUNT ______________________________ ACCOUNT NO. __________

DATE	DESCRIPTION	POST. REF.	DEBIT	CREDIT	BALANCE	
					DEBIT	CREDIT

ACCOUNT ______________________________ ACCOUNT NO. __________

DATE	DESCRIPTION	POST. REF.	DEBIT	CREDIT	BALANCE	
					DEBIT	CREDIT

Name

PROBLEM 6.4A or 6.4B

ACCOUNT NAME	TRIAL BALANCE		ADJUSTMENTS	
	DEBIT	CREDIT	DEBIT	CREDIT

Name ____________________

PROBLEM 6.4A or 6.4B (continued)

ADJUSTED TRIAL BALANCE		INCOME STATEMENT		BALANCE SHEET		
DEBIT	CREDIT	DEBIT	CREDIT	DEBIT	CREDIT	
						1
						2
						3
						4
						5
						6
						7
						8
						9
						10
						11
						12
						13
						14
						15
						16
						17
						18
						19
						20
						21
						22
						23
						24
						25
						26
						27
						28
						29
						30
						31
						32

Name ____________________

PROBLEM 6.4A or 6.4B (continued)

GENERAL JOURNAL PAGE ______

	DATE		DESCRIPTION	POST. REF.	DEBIT	CREDIT	
1							1
2							2
3							3
4							4
5							5
6							6
7							7
8							8
9							9
10							10
11							11
12							12
13							13

GENERAL JOURNAL PAGE ______

	DATE		DESCRIPTION	POST. REF.	DEBIT	CREDIT	
1							1
2							2
3							3
4							4
5							5
6							6
7							7
8							8
9							9
10							10
11							11
12							12
13							13
14							14
15							15
16							16
17							17
18							18

Name

PROBLEM 6.4A or 6.4B (continued)

GENERAL LEDGER

ACCOUNT **Supplies** ACCOUNT NO. **121**

DATE		DESCRIPTION	POST. REF.	DEBIT	CREDIT	BALANCE DEBIT	BALANCE CREDIT

ACCOUNT **Prepaid Advertising** ACCOUNT NO. **131**

DATE		DESCRIPTION	POST. REF.	DEBIT	CREDIT	BALANCE DEBIT	BALANCE CREDIT

ACCOUNT **Accumulated Depreciation—** ACCOUNT NO. **142**

DATE		DESCRIPTION	POST. REF.	DEBIT	CREDIT	BALANCE DEBIT	BALANCE CREDIT

ACCOUNT **Capital** ACCOUNT NO. **301**

DATE		DESCRIPTION	POST. REF.	DEBIT	CREDIT	BALANCE DEBIT	BALANCE CREDIT

ACCOUNT **Drawing** ACCOUNT NO. **302**

DATE		DESCRIPTION	POST. REF.	DEBIT	CREDIT	BALANCE DEBIT	BALANCE CREDIT

Name

PROBLEM 6.4A or 6.4B (continued)

GENERAL LEDGER

ACCOUNT **Income Summary** ACCOUNT NO. **399**

DATE	DESCRIPTION	POST. REF.	DEBIT	CREDIT	BALANCE DEBIT	BALANCE CREDIT

ACCOUNT **Fees Income** ACCOUNT NO. **401**

DATE	DESCRIPTION	POST. REF.	DEBIT	CREDIT	BALANCE DEBIT	BALANCE CREDIT

GENERAL LEDGER

ACCOUNT **Salaries Expense** ACCOUNT NO. **511**

DATE	DESCRIPTION	POST. REF.	DEBIT	CREDIT	BALANCE DEBIT	BALANCE CREDIT

ACCOUNT **Utilities Expense** ACCOUNT NO. **514**

DATE	DESCRIPTION	POST. REF.	DEBIT	CREDIT	BALANCE DEBIT	BALANCE CREDIT

ACCOUNT **Supplies Expense** ACCOUNT NO. **517**

DATE	DESCRIPTION	POST. REF.	DEBIT	CREDIT	BALANCE DEBIT	BALANCE CREDIT

Name

PROBLEM 6.4A or 6.4B (continued)

ACCOUNT **Depreciation Expense—** ACCOUNT NO. **523**

DATE	DESCRIPTION	POST. REF.	DEBIT	CREDIT	BALANCE DEBIT	BALANCE CREDIT

ACCOUNT **Advertising Expense** ACCOUNT NO. **526**

DATE	DESCRIPTION	POST. REF.	DEBIT	CREDIT	BALANCE DEBIT	BALANCE CREDIT

ACCOUNT NAME	DEBIT	CREDIT

Analyze:

Name

CRITICAL THINKING PROBLEM 6.1

21st Century Fashions
Worksheet
Month Ended December 31, 2016

ACCOUNT NAME	TRIAL BALANCE DEBIT	TRIAL BALANCE CREDIT	ADJUSTMENTS DEBIT	ADJUSTMENTS CREDIT
Cash	81 6 0 0 00			
Accounts Receivable	18 0 0 0 00			
Supplies	14 4 0 0 00			(a) 7 2 0 0 00
Prepaid Insurance	21 6 0 0 00			(b) 4 8 0 0 00
Machinery	168 0 0 0 00			
Accumulated Depreciation—Machinery				(c) 2 4 0 0 00
Accounts Payable		27 0 0 0 00		
Carolyn Davis, Capital		149 1 6 0 00		
Carolyn Davis, Drawing	12 0 0 0 00			
Fees Income		165 0 0 0 00		
Supplies Expense			(a) 7 2 0 0 00	
Insurance Expense			(b) 4 8 0 0 00	
Salaries Expense	22 2 0 0 00			
Depreciation Expense—Machinery			(c) 2 4 0 0 00	
Utilities Expense	3 3 6 0 00			
Totals	341 1 6 0 00	341 1 6 0 00	14 4 0 0 00	14 4 0 0 00
Net Income				

Name

CRITICAL THINKING PROBLEM 6.1 (continued)

ADJUSTED TRIAL BALANCE		INCOME STATEMENT		BALANCE SHEET	
DEBIT	CREDIT	DEBIT	CREDIT	DEBIT	CREDIT

Name

CRITICAL THINKING PROBLEM 6.1 (continued)

Name

CRITICAL THINKING PROBLEM 6.1 (continued)

GENERAL JOURNAL

PAGE

	DATE		DESCRIPTION	POST. REF.	DEBIT	CREDIT	
1							1
2							2
3							3
4							4
5							5
6							6
7							7
8							8
9							9
10							10
11							11
12							12
13							13
14							14
15							15
16							16

Name

CRITICAL THINKING PROBLEM 6.1 (continued)

GENERAL JOURNAL PAGE

	DATE		DESCRIPTION	POST. REF.	DEBIT	CREDIT	
1							1
2							2
3							3
4							4
5							5
6							6
7							7
8							8
9							9
10							10
11							11
12							12
13							13
14							14
15							15
16							16
17							17
18							18

ACCOUNT NAME	DEBIT	CREDIT

Analyze:

Name

CRITICAL THINKING PROBLEM 6.2

1.

2.

GENERAL JOURNAL

PAGE

	DATE		DESCRIPTION	POST. REF.	DEBIT	CREDIT	
1							1
2							2
3							3
4							4
5							5
6							6

3.

Name

CRITICAL THINKING PROBLEM 6.2 (continued)

Chapter 6 Practice Test Answer Key

Part A True-False

1. F
2. T
3. F
4. T
5. F
6. F
7. T
8. F
9. F
10. T

Part B Matching

1. d
2. c
3. e
4. b
5. a

Name ____________________

MINI-PRACTICE SET 1

Service Business Accounting Cycle

GENERAL JOURNAL

PAGE ______

	DATE		DESCRIPTION	POST. REF.	DEBIT	CREDIT	
1							1
2							2
3							3
4							4
5							5
6							6
7							7
8							8
9							9
10							10
11							11
12							12
13							13
14							14
15							15
16							16
17							17
18							18
19							19
20							20
21							21
22							22
23							23
24							24
25							25
26							26
27							27
28							28
29							29
30							30
31							31
32							32
33							33
34							34

 Name

GENERAL JOURNAL PAGE

DATE		DESCRIPTION	POST. REF.	DEBIT	CREDIT

 Name

GENERAL JOURNAL

PAGE

	DATE	DESCRIPTION	POST. REF.	DEBIT	CREDIT	
1						1
2						2
3						3
4						4
5						5
6						6
7						7
8						8
9						9
10						10
11						11
12						12
13						13
14						14
15						15
16						16
17						17
18						18
19						19
20						20
21						21
22						22
23						23
24						24
25						25
26						26
27						27
28						28
29						29
30						30
31						31
32						32
33						33
34						34
35						35
36						36
37						37
38						38
39						39

 Name ____________________

GENERAL JOURNAL

PAGE ______

DATE	DESCRIPTION	POST. REF.	DEBIT	CREDIT

 Name

GENERAL LEDGER

ACCOUNT ACCOUNT NO.

DATE		DESCRIPTION	POST. REF.	DEBIT	CREDIT	BALANCE	
						DEBIT	CREDIT

ACCOUNT ACCOUNT NO.

DATE		DESCRIPTION	POST. REF.	DEBIT	CREDIT	BALANCE	
						DEBIT	CREDIT

 Name ____________

GENERAL LEDGER

ACCOUNT ____________ ACCOUNT NO. ______

DATE	DESCRIPTION	POST. REF.	DEBIT	CREDIT	BALANCE DEBIT	BALANCE CREDIT

ACCOUNT ____________ ACCOUNT NO. ______

DATE	DESCRIPTION	POST. REF.	DEBIT	CREDIT	BALANCE DEBIT	BALANCE CREDIT

ACCOUNT ____________ ACCOUNT NO. ______

DATE	DESCRIPTION	POST. REF.	DEBIT	CREDIT	BALANCE DEBIT	BALANCE CREDIT

ACCOUNT ____________ ACCOUNT NO. ______

DATE	DESCRIPTION	POST. REF.	DEBIT	CREDIT	BALANCE DEBIT	BALANCE CREDIT

ACCOUNT ____________ ACCOUNT NO. ______

DATE	DESCRIPTION	POST. REF.	DEBIT	CREDIT	BALANCE DEBIT	BALANCE CREDIT

 Name ____________________

GENERAL LEDGER

ACCOUNT ____________________ ACCOUNT NO. ________

DATE		DESCRIPTION	POST. REF.	DEBIT	CREDIT	BALANCE	
						DEBIT	CREDIT

ACCOUNT ____________________ ACCOUNT NO. ________

DATE		DESCRIPTION	POST. REF.	DEBIT	CREDIT	BALANCE	
						DEBIT	CREDIT

ACCOUNT ____________________ ACCOUNT NO. ________

DATE		DESCRIPTION	POST. REF.	DEBIT	CREDIT	BALANCE	
						DEBIT	CREDIT

ACCOUNT ____________________ ACCOUNT NO. ________

DATE		DESCRIPTION	POST. REF.	DEBIT	CREDIT	BALANCE	
						DEBIT	CREDIT

 Name ____________________

GENERAL LEDGER

ACCOUNT ____________________ ACCOUNT NO. ________

DATE	DESCRIPTION	POST. REF.	DEBIT	CREDIT	BALANCE	
					DEBIT	CREDIT

ACCOUNT ____________________ ACCOUNT NO. ________

DATE	DESCRIPTION	POST. REF.	DEBIT	CREDIT	BALANCE	
					DEBIT	CREDIT

ACCOUNT ____________________ ACCOUNT NO. ________

DATE	DESCRIPTION	POST. REF.	DEBIT	CREDIT	BALANCE	
					DEBIT	CREDIT

ACCOUNT ____________________ ACCOUNT NO. ________

DATE	DESCRIPTION	POST. REF.	DEBIT	CREDIT	BALANCE	
					DEBIT	CREDIT

ACCOUNT ____________________ ACCOUNT NO. ________

DATE	DESCRIPTION	POST. REF.	DEBIT	CREDIT	BALANCE	
					DEBIT	CREDIT

GENERAL LEDGER

ACCOUNT ______ ACCOUNT NO. ______

DATE	DESCRIPTION	POST. REF.	DEBIT	CREDIT	BALANCE	
					DEBIT	CREDIT

ACCOUNT ______ ACCOUNT NO. ______

DATE	DESCRIPTION	POST. REF.	DEBIT	CREDIT	BALANCE	
					DEBIT	CREDIT

ACCOUNT ______ ACCOUNT NO. ______

DATE	DESCRIPTION	POST. REF.	DEBIT	CREDIT	BALANCE	
					DEBIT	CREDIT

ACCOUNT ______ ACCOUNT NO. ______

DATE	DESCRIPTION	POST. REF.	DEBIT	CREDIT	BALANCE	
					DEBIT	CREDIT

ACCOUNT ______ ACCOUNT NO. ______

DATE	DESCRIPTION	POST. REF.	DEBIT	CREDIT	BALANCE	
					DEBIT	CREDIT

MINI-PRACTICE SET 1 (continued)

Name ____________________

	ACCOUNT NAME	TRIAL BALANCE		ADJUSTMENTS	
		DEBIT	CREDIT	DEBIT	CREDIT
1					
2					
3					
4					
5					
6					
7					
8					
9					
10					
11					
12					
13					
14					
15					
16					
17					
18					
19					
20					
21					
22					
23					
24					
25					
26					
27					
28					
29					
30					
31					
32					
33					
34					
35					
36					
37					

Name ______________________

ADJUSTED TRIAL BALANCE		INCOME STATEMENT		BALANCE SHEET	
DEBIT	CREDIT	DEBIT	CREDIT	DEBIT	CREDIT

MINI-PRACTICE SET 1 (continued)

Name

 Name ____________________

ACCOUNT NAME	DEBIT	CREDIT

 Name

Analyze:

CHAPTER 7

Accounting for Sales, Accounts Receivable, and Cash Receipts

STUDY GUIDE

Understanding the Chapter

Objectives

1. Record sales on account, credit card sales, sales returns, and cash receipt transactions in a general journal. **2.** Compute trade discounts. **3.** Compute and record cash discounts on sales. **4.** Post from the general journal to the general ledger accounts and to the subsidiary ledger. **5.** Prepare a schedule of accounts receivable. **6.** Record the payment of sales taxes. **7.** Define the accounting terms new to this chapter.

Reading Assignment

Read Chapter 7 in the textbook. Complete the textbook Section Self Review as you finish reading each section of the chapter, and the Comprehensive Self Review at the end of the chapter. Refer to the Chapter 7 Glossary or to the Glossary at the end of the book to find definitions for terms that are not familiar to you.

Activities

- ❑ **Thinking Critically** — Answer the *Thinking Critically* questions for Kellogg Company.
- ❑ **Discussion Questions** — Answer each assigned discussion question in Chapter 7.
- ❑ **Exercises** — Complete each assigned exercise in Chapter 7. Use the forms provided in this SGWP. The objectives covered by an exercise are given after the exercise number. If you need help with an exercise, review the portion of the chapter related to the objective(s) covered.
- ❑ **Problems A/B** — Complete each assigned problem in Chapter 7. Use the forms provided in this SGWP. The objectives covered by a problem are given after the problem number. If you need help with a problem, review the portion of the chapter related to the objective(s) covered.
- ❑ **Critical Thinking Problems** — Complete critical thinking problems 7.1 and 7.2 as assigned. Use the forms provided in this SGWP.
- ❑ **Business Connections** — Complete the Business Connections activities as assigned to gain a deeper understanding of Chapter 7 concepts.

Practice Tests

Complete the Practice Tests, which cover the main points in your reading assignment. Compare your answers with those in the Practice Test Answer Key for Chapter 7 at the end of this chapter. If you have answered any questions incorrectly, review the related section of the text.

Part A True-False *For each of the following statements, circle T in the answer column if the statement is true and F if the statement is false.*

T F 1. Both the **Credit Card Expense** and **Sales Discounts** accounts have normal debit balances.

T F 2. The trade discount is a subtraction from list price to calculate the net sales price.

T F 3. Sales less **Sales Returns and Allowances** less **Sales Discounts** equals net sales.

T F 4. Both Sales Returns and Allowances and Purchases Discounts are classified as contra-revenue accounts.

T F 5. If the shipping terms are FOB Destination, the buyer will pay the freight charges.

T F 6. If credit terms of sale are 1/10, n/30, the buyer has thirty days after the date of the invoice to take advantage of the cash discount.

T F 7. **Sales Tax Payable** is an asset account with a normal credit balance.

T F 8. To record the return of merchandise by the buyer to the seller in the seller's general journal, debit **Sales Returns and Allowances**, and credit **Accounts Payable**.

T F 9. When a customer returns goods on which sales tax was charged, the firm gives credit for the price of the goods and for the sales tax.

T F 10. The amount of each credit sale is posted daily to the customer's account in the accounts receivable subsidiary ledger.

T F 11. To ensure accuracy, the total of all customers' accounts in the accounts receivable ledger is compared with the balance of the **Accounts Receivable** account in the general ledger.

T F 12. The accountant must keep an individual record of transactions with each customer to answer questions from managers and salespeople of the company, from customers themselves, and to follow up amounts overdue from customers.

T F 13. Sales on credit require debits to **Accounts Payable**.

T F 14. A credit sale made on a credit card issued by a credit card company is accounted for in the same way as a credit card sale made using a bank credit card.

T F 15. The **Sales** account may be credited for a sale made for cash or on account.

T F 16. Company B is a customer of Company S. An accounts receivable clerk employed by Company S wishes to check the balance owed by Company B. This balance would be found in the Accounts Payable subsidiary ledger maintained by Company S.

T F 17. On June 10, the Seller Company sold merchandise on account to the Buyer Company for $900, terms 1/10, n/30, FOB Shipping Point. Freight charges of $50 were prepaid by the Seller Company and added to the invoice. On June 15, the Buyer Company returned $50 of defective merchandise. On June 19, the Buyer Company paid the remaining amount due. The Seller Company would have received $891.50 as payment in full.

T F 18. Refer to Question #17 above. The entry to record the transaction of June 19 on the books of the Seller Company would have included a credit to **Sales Discounts**.

T F 19. On April 4, the Seller Company sold merchandise on account to Buyer Company for $1,000, terms 2/10, n/30, FOB Destination. The Buyer Company returned $100 of merchandise on April 6, and then paid the remaining amount due on April 10th. Buyer Company should pay $880 on April 10th.

T F 20. Sales returns and allowances effectively increase a company's revenues.

STUDY GUIDE

Part B Matching *For each numbered item, choose the matching term from the box and write the identifying letter in the answer column.*

a. Bank credit cards
b. Accounts receivable ledger
c. Open-account credit
d. Sales tax payable
e. Business credit card
f. Sales return or allowance
g. Trade discount

G 1. A reduction in price, based on volume purchased, given by wholesalers to retailers who buy goods for resale.

C 2. The type of credit usually given by a business on the basis of the personal knowledge of the customer.

E 3. Identification cards given by some businesses to their customers who have established credit.

A 4. Identification cards used by some banks to individuals for use in making credit card purchases at participating businesses.

B 5. A subsidiary ledger with individual accounts for all credit customers.

D 6. A liability account for recording a tax levied by some states on certain retail sales.

F 7. A reduction in the amount charged to a customer who has received defective goods or services.

Part C Exercise *Answer each question about the accounts receivable subsidiary ledger account shown below.*

ACCOUNTS RECEIVABLE SUBSIDIARY LEDGER

NAME **Andrew Cho** TERMS

ADDRESS **1891 Windsor Drive, Dallas, TX 75623-6998**

DATE		DESCRIPTION	POST. REF.	DEBIT	CREDIT	BALANCE DEBIT	BALANCE CREDIT
2016							
Jan.	**1**	**Balance**	✔			**500 00**	
	4	**Sales Slip 101**	**J1**	**60 00**		**560 00**	
	7	**Sales Slip 167**	**J1**	**90 00**		**650 00**	
	17		**J1**		**85 00**	**565 00**	

1. Where did the $500 entry come from?

Carried over from December 2015

2. How could you find a complete description of the $60 charge on January 4?

from the Sales Slip 101.

3. What was the probable reason for the $85 entry on January 17? How can you find out for sure?

Sales Return. Ref to 1/17

Part D Exercise

On April 1, Alenikov Disturbutors sold merchandise on account to Kisling's Kitchens for $3,500 on Invoice 1001, terms 2/10, n/30. On April 5, Alenikov Disturbutors issued Credit Memorandum 102 to Kisling Kitchens for damaged merchandise returned, $250. On April 10, payment was received in full from Kisling's Kitchens, less the return of April 5, and less the discount.

Required: Record the transactions on April 1, 5 and 10. Use 14 as the journal page number. Do not post the journal entries to the general ledger. The "Post. Ref." column is excluded in the general journal form below.

GENERAL JOURNAL PAGE ________

	DATE		DESCRIPTION	POST. REF.	DEBIT	CREDIT	
1							1
2							2
3							3
4							4
5							5
6							6
7							7
8							8
9							9
10							10
11							11
12							12
13							13
14							14
15							15
16							16
17							17
18							18

Demonstration Problem

Vanessa's Gift Shop sells cards, supplies, and various holiday greeting cards. Sales to retail customers are subject to a 8% sales tax. The firm sells its merchandise for cash; to customers using bank credit cards, such as MasterCard and VISA; to customers using American Express; and to certain customers on credit. The bank credit cards charge a 2% fee. American Express charges a 3% fee. Vanessa's Gift Shop also grants trade discounts to certain wholesale customers who place large orders. These orders are not subject to sales tax. During April 2016, Vanessa's Gift Shop engaged in the following transactions.

DATE	TRANSACTIONS
2016	
April 1	Sold crystal goods to Great Kitchens, a wholesale customer. The list price is $4,200, with a 30% trade discount. This sale is not subject to sales tax. Issued Invoice 5950 with terms of n/15.
15	Recorded cash sales for the period from April 1 to April 15 of $9,200 plus sales tax of $736.
15	Recorded sales for the period from April 1 to April 15 to customers using bank credit cards of $12,900 plus sales tax of $1,032. (Record the 2% credit card expense at this time.)
16	Received a check from Great Kitchens in payment of Invoice 5950 dated April 1.
16	Sold merchandise to customers using American Express for $10,000 plus sales tax of $800.
17	Sold a set of Roman statues to Jim Peterson, a wholesale customer, for $5,000. The list price is $8,900, with a 25% trade discount. This sale is not subject to sales tax. Issued Invoice 5951 with terms of n/15.
20	Received payment from American Express for amount billed on April 16, less a 3% credit card expense.
27	Received payment in full from Jim Peterson for the sale of April 17, less appropriate cash discount.
28	Recorded cash sales for the period from April 16 to April 30 of $8,050 plus sales tax of $644.
28	Recorded sales for the period from April 16 to April 30 to customers using bank credit cards of $11,800 plus sales tax of $944. (Record the 2% credit card expense at this time.)
30	Sold merchandise to customers using American Express for $10,200 plus sales tax of $816.
30	Received a check from Victoria Home Products for $1,440 in payment of invoice 5948 of March 29.

Instructions

1. Open the general ledger accounts indicated below and enter the balances as of April 1, 2016.
2. Open the accounts receivable ledger accounts indicated below. Enter the April 1 balances for Southwest Living and Victoria Home Products.
3. Record the transactions in a general journal. Use 10 as the journal page number.
4. Post the entries from the general journal to the appropriate accounts in the general ledger.
5. Post the entries from the general journal to the accounts receivable subsidiary ledger.
6. Prepare a schedule of accounts receivable at April 30, 2016.

General Ledger Accounts

101 Cash, $23,830 Dr.
121 Accounts Receivable, $2,940 Dr.
222 Sales Tax Payable
401 Sales
521 Credit Card Expense

Accounts Receivable Ledger Accounts

American Express
Great Kitchens
Jim Peterson
Southwest Living, $1,500
Victoria Home Products, $1,440

SOLUTION

GENERAL JOURNAL PAGE 10

DATE		DESCRIPTION	POST. REF.	DEBIT	CREDIT
2016					
April	1	Accounts Receivable/Great Kitchens	121/✓	2940 00	
		Sales [$4,200 – ($4,200 x 30%)]	401		2940 00
		Sold crystal goods on credit to Great Kitchens,			
		Invoice 5950, n/15			
	15	Cash ($9,200 + $736)	101	9936 00	
		Sales	401		9200 00
		Sales Tax Payable	222		736 00
		Record cash sales, April 1 – 15			
	15	Credit Card Expense ($12,900 + $1,032) × 2%	521	278 64	
		Cash ($12,900 + $1,032 – $278.64)	101	13653 36	
		Sales	401		12900 00
		Sales Tax Payable	222		1032 00
		Record credit card sales, April 1 – 15			
	16	Cash	101	2940 00	
		Accounts Receivable/Great Kitchens	121/✓		2940 00
		Received payment on account, Invoice 5950			
	16	Accounts Receivable/American Express	121/✓	10800 00	
		Sales	401		10000 00
		Sales Tax Payable	222		800 00
		Sold merchandise to customers using			
		American Express			
	17	Accounts Receivable / Jim Peterson	121/✓	6675 00	
		Sales	401		6675 00
		Sold a set of Roman statues on credit to			
		Michael Gibrone, Invoice 5951, 2/10, n/30			
	20	Credit Card Expense ($10,800 × 3%)	521	324 00	
		Cash ($10,800 – $324)	101	10476 00	
		Accounts Receivable/American Express	121/✓		10800 00
		Received payment from American Express for			
		amount billed on April 16			

SOLUTION (continued)

GENERAL JOURNAL PAGE 11

DATE		DESCRIPTION	POST. REF.	DEBIT	CREDIT
2016					
April	27	Cash	101	6,675.00	
		Accounts Receivable/Jim Peterson	121 / ✓		6,675.00
		Received payment on account for Invoice 5951			
	28	Cash ($8,050 + $644)	101	8,694.00	
		Sales	401		8,050.00
		Sales Tax Payable	222		644.00
		Record cash sales, April 16 – 30			
	28	Credit Card Expense ($11,800 + $944) × 2%	521	254.88	
		Cash ($11,800 + $944 – $254.88)	101	12,489.12	
		Sales	401		11,800.00
		Sales Tax Payable	222		944.00
		Record credit card sales, April 16 – 30			

SOLUTION (continued)

GENERAL JOURNAL

PAGE 12

DATE		DESCRIPTION	POST. REF.	DEBIT	CREDIT
2016					
April	30	Accounts Receivable/American Express	121/✓	11,016.00	
		Sales	401		10,200.00
		Sales Tax Payable	222		816.00
		Sold merchandise to customers using			
		American Express			
	30	Cash	101	1,440.00	
		Accounts Receivable/Victoria Home Products	121/✓		1,440.00
		Received payment on account for Invoice 5948			

GENERAL LEDGER

ACCOUNT Cash ACCOUNT NO. 101

DATE		DESCRIPTION	POST. REF.	DEBIT	CREDIT	BALANCE DEBIT	BALANCE CREDIT
2016							
April	1	Balance	✓			23,830.00	
	15		J10	9,936.00		33,766.00	
	15		J10	13,653.36		47,419.36	
	16		J10	2,940.00		50,359.36	
	20		J11	10,476.00		60,835.36	
	27		J11	6,675.00		67,510.36	
	28		J11	8,694.00		76,204.36	
	28		J11	12,489.12		88,693.48	
	30		J12	1,440.00		90,133.48	

STUDY GUIDE

SOLUTION (continued)

ACCOUNT **Accounts Receivable** ACCOUNT NO. **121**

DATE		DESCRIPTION	POST. REF.	DEBIT	CREDIT	BALANCE DEBIT	BALANCE CREDIT
2016							
April	**1**	**Balance**	✔			2,940.00	
	1		**J10**	2,940.00		5,880.00	
	16		**J10**		2,940.00	2,940.00	
	16		**J10**	10,800.00		13,740.00	
	17		**J10**	6,675.00		20,415.00	
	20		**J11**		10,800.00	9,615.00	
	27		**J11**		6,675.00	2,940.00	
	30		**J12**	11,016.00		13,956.00	
	30		**J12**		1,440.00	12,516.00	

ACCOUNT **Sales Tax Payable** ACCOUNT NO. **222**

DATE		DESCRIPTION	POST. REF.	DEBIT	CREDIT	BALANCE DEBIT	BALANCE CREDIT
2016							
April	**15**		**J10**		736.00		736.00
	15		**J10**		1,032.00		1,768.00
	16		**J10**		800.00		2,568.00
	28		**J11**		644.00		3,212.00
	28		**J11**		944.00		4,156.00
	30		**J12**		816.00		4,972.00

SOLUTION (continued)

ACCOUNT Sales ACCOUNT NO. 401

DATE		DESCRIPTION	POST. REF.	DEBIT	CREDIT	BALANCE DEBIT	BALANCE CREDIT
2016							
April	1		J10		2,940.00		2,940.00
	15		J10		9,200.00		12,140.00
	15		J10		12,900.00		25,040.00
	16		J10		10,000.00		35,040.00
	17		J10		6,675.00		41,715.00
	28		J11		8,050.00		49,765.00
	28		J11		11,800.00		61,565.00
	30		J12		10,200.00		71,765.00

ACCOUNT Credit Card Expense ACCOUNT NO. 521

DATE		DESCRIPTION	POST. REF.	DEBIT	CREDIT	BALANCE DEBIT	BALANCE CREDIT
2016							
April	15		J10	278.64		278.64	
	20		J11	324.00		602.64	
	28		J11	254.88		857.52	

ACCOUNTS RECEIVABLE SUBSIDIARY LEDGER

NAME American Express

ADDRESS

DATE		DESCRIPTION	POST. REF.	DEBIT	CREDIT	BALANCE
2016						
April	16		J10	10,800.00		10,800.00
	20		J10		10,800.00	-0-
	30		J12	11,016.00		11,016.00

STUDY GUIDE

SOLUTION (continued)

NAME Great Kitchens
ADDRESS

DATE		DESCRIPTION	POST. REF.	DEBIT	CREDIT	BALANCE
2016						
April	1	Invoice 5950	J10	2 9 4 0 00		2 9 4 0 00
	16		J10		2 9 4 0 00	- 0 -

NAME Jim Peterson
ADDRESS

DATE		DESCRIPTION	POST. REF.	DEBIT	CREDIT	BALANCE
2016						
April	17	Invoice 5951	J10	6 6 7 5 00		6 6 7 5 00
	26		J11		6 6 7 5 00	- 0 -

NAME Southwest Living
ADDRESS

DATE		DESCRIPTION	POST. REF.	DEBIT	CREDIT	BALANCE
2016						
April	1	Balance	✔			1 5 0 0 00

NAME Victoria Home Products
ADDRESS

DATE		DESCRIPTION	POST. REF.	DEBIT	CREDIT	BALANCE
2016						
April	16	Balance	✔			1 4 4 0 00
	30		J12		1 4 4 0 00	- 0 -

STUDY GUIDE

SOLUTION (continued)

Vanessa's Gift Shop
Schedule of Accounts Receivable
April 30, 2016

American Express	11 0 1 6 00
Great Kitchens	- 0 -
Jim Peterson	- 0 -
Southwest Living	1 5 0 0 00
Victoria Home Products	- 0 -
Total	12 5 1 6 00

WORKING PAPERS

Name ______________________________

EXERCISE 7.1

____ Sales

____ Sales Returns and Allowances

____ Sales Discounts

____ Credit Card Expense

____ Sales Tax Payable

EXERCISE 7.2

GENERAL JOURNAL

PAGE ______

	DATE	DESCRIPTION	POST. REF.	DEBIT	CREDIT	
1						1
2						2
3						3
4						4
5						5
6						6
7						7
8						8
9						9
10						10
11						11
12						12
13						13
14						14

Name ________________________________

EXERCISE 7.3

GENERAL JOURNAL

PAGE ________

DATE		DESCRIPTION	POST. REF.	DEBIT	CREDIT

Name ____________________

EXERCISE 7.4

GENERAL JOURNAL PAGE ______

DATE	DESCRIPTION	POST. REF.	DEBIT	CREDIT

Name ____________________

EXERCISE 7.5

GENERAL JOURNAL PAGE ______

	DATE	DESCRIPTION	POST. REF.	DEBIT	CREDIT	
1						1
2						2
3						3
4						4
5						5
6						6
7						7
8						8
9						9
10						10
11						11
12						12
13						13
14						14
15						15
16						16
17						17
18						18
19						19
20						20
21						21
22						22
23						23
24						24
25						25
26						26
27						27
28						28
29						29

EXERCISE 7.6

1. ________
2. ________
3. ________

Name

EXERCISE 7.7

1.

2.

3.

EXERCISE 7.8

GENERAL JOURNAL

PAGE

	DATE		DESCRIPTION	POST. REF.	DEBIT	CREDIT	
1							1
2							2
3							3
4							4
5							5
6							6
7							7
8							8
9							9
10							10
11							11
12							12
13							13
14							14
15							15

Name

EXERCISE 7.9

GENERAL JOURNAL

PAGE 40

DATE		DESCRIPTION	POST. REF.	DEBIT	CREDIT
2013					
Jan.	8	Cash		540 00	
		Accounts Receivable/John Gibrone			540 00
		Received partial payment on account from			
		John Gibrone			
	20	Sales Returns and Allowances		100 00	
		Sales Tax Payable		8 00	
		Accounts Receivable/Jim Garcia			108 00
		Accepted return of defective merchandise, Credit			
		Memorandum 121; original sale made on Sales			
		Slip 11102 of December 27, 2012			

GENERAL LEDGER

ACCOUNT Accounts Receivable ACCOUNT NO. 111

DATE		DESCRIPTION	POST. REF.	DEBIT	CREDIT	BALANCE DEBIT	BALANCE CREDIT
2013							
Jan.	1	Balance	✔			8,640 00	

ACCOUNTS RECEIVABLE SUBSIDIARY LEDGER

NAME Jim Garcia

ADDRESS

DATE		DESCRIPTION	POST. REF.	DEBIT	CREDIT	BALANCE
2013						
Jan.	1	Balance	✔			2,160 00

EXERCISE 7.9 (continued)

NAME John Gibrone
ADDRESS

DATE		DESCRIPTION	POST. REF.	DEBIT	CREDIT	BALANCE
2013						
Jan.	1	Balance	✔			5,400.00

NAME June Lin
ADDRESS

DATE		DESCRIPTION	POST. REF.	DEBIT	CREDIT	BALANCE
2013						
Jan.	1	Balance	✔			1,080.00

EXERCISE 7.10

1.

2. Should the total of your accounts receivable schedule agree with the balance of the accounts receivable account in the general ledger at January 31, 2013?

Name

PROBLEM 7.1A

GENERAL JOURNAL

PAGE

DATE		DESCRIPTION	POST. REF.	DEBIT	CREDIT

Name

PROBLEM 7.1A (continued)

GENERAL JOURNAL

PAGE

	DATE		DESCRIPTION	POST. REF.	DEBIT	CREDIT	
1							1
2							2
3							3
4							4
5							5
6							6
7							7
8							8
9							9
10							10
11							11

GENERAL LEDGER

ACCOUNT ACCOUNT NO.

DATE		DESCRIPTION	POST. REF.	DEBIT	CREDIT	BALANCE	
						DEBIT	CREDIT

ACCOUNT ACCOUNT NO.

DATE		DESCRIPTION	POST. REF.	DEBIT	CREDIT	BALANCE	
						DEBIT	CREDIT

Name

PROBLEM 7.1A (continued)

ACCOUNT ______ ACCOUNT NO. ______

DATE		DESCRIPTION	POST. REF.	DEBIT	CREDIT	BALANCE DEBIT	BALANCE CREDIT

ACCOUNT ______ ACCOUNT NO. ______

DATE		DESCRIPTION	POST. REF.	DEBIT	CREDIT	BALANCE DEBIT	BALANCE CREDIT

Analyze: ______

Name ____________________

PROBLEM 7.2A

GENERAL JOURNAL

PAGE ______

DATE		DESCRIPTION	POST. REF.	DEBIT	CREDIT

Name

PROBLEM 7.2A (continued)

GENERAL JOURNAL

PAGE

	DATE		DESCRIPTION	POST. REF.	DEBIT	CREDIT	
1							1
2							2
3							3
4							4
5							5
6							6
7							7
8							8
9							9
10							10
11							11
12							12
13							13
14							14
15							15
16							16
17							17
18							18
19							19
20							20
21							21
22							22
23							23
24							24
25							25
26							26
27							27
28							28
29							29
30							30
31							31
32							32

Analyze:

Name

PROBLEM 7.3A

GENERAL LEDGER

ACCOUNT ACCOUNT NO.

DATE		DESCRIPTION	POST. REF.	DEBIT	CREDIT	BALANCE DEBIT	BALANCE CREDIT

ACCOUNT ACCOUNT NO.

DATE		DESCRIPTION	POST. REF.	DEBIT	CREDIT	BALANCE DEBIT	BALANCE CREDIT

Name ______________________________

PROBLEM 7.3A (continued)

GENERAL LEDGER

ACCOUNT ______________________________ ACCOUNT NO. ________

DATE		DESCRIPTION	POST. REF.	DEBIT	CREDIT	BALANCE DEBIT	BALANCE CREDIT

ACCOUNT ______________________________ ACCOUNT NO. ________

DATE		DESCRIPTION	POST. REF.	DEBIT	CREDIT	BALANCE DEBIT	BALANCE CREDIT

ACCOUNT ______________________________ ACCOUNT NO. ________

DATE		DESCRIPTION	POST. REF.	DEBIT	CREDIT	BALANCE DEBIT	BALANCE CREDIT

Name

PROBLEM 7.3A (continued)

ACCOUNTS RECEIVABLE SUBSIDIARY LEDGER

NAME
ADDRESS

DATE		DESCRIPTION	POST. REF.	DEBIT	CREDIT	BALANCE

NAME
ADDRESS

DATE		DESCRIPTION	POST. REF.	DEBIT	CREDIT	BALANCE

NAME
ADDRESS

DATE		DESCRIPTION	POST. REF.	DEBIT	CREDIT	BALANCE

NAME
ADDRESS

DATE		DESCRIPTION	POST. REF.	DEBIT	CREDIT	BALANCE

Name

PROBLEM 7.3A (continued)

ACCOUNTS RECEIVABLE SUBSIDIARY LEDGER

NAME

ADDRESS

DATE		DESCRIPTION	POST. REF.	DEBIT	CREDIT	BALANCE

Compare the balance of the Accounts Receivable control account with the total of the schedule.

Analyze:

Name ____________________

PROBLEM 7.4A

GENERAL JOURNAL PAGE ______

DATE	DESCRIPTION	POST. REF.	DEBIT	CREDIT

Name

PROBLEM 7.4A (continued)

GENERAL JOURNAL

PAGE

DATE	DESCRIPTION	POST. REF.	DEBIT	CREDIT

Name ____________________

PROBLEM 7.4A (continued)

GENERAL JOURNAL PAGE ______

	DATE		DESCRIPTION	POST. REF.	DEBIT	CREDIT	
1							1
2							2
3							3
4							4
5							5
6							6
7							7
8							8
9							9
10							10
11							11
12							12
13							13
14							14
15							15

Analyze:

PROBLEM 7.5A

GENERAL LEDGER

ACCOUNT ____________________ ACCOUNT NO. ______

DATE		DESCRIPTION	POST. REF.	DEBIT	CREDIT	BALANCE	
						DEBIT	CREDIT

Name ____________________

PROBLEM 7.5A (continued)

GENERAL LEDGER

ACCOUNT ____________________ ACCOUNT NO. ________

DATE	DESCRIPTION	POST. REF.	DEBIT	CREDIT	BALANCE	
					DEBIT	CREDIT

ACCOUNT ____________________ ACCOUNT NO. ________

DATE	DESCRIPTION	POST. REF.	DEBIT	CREDIT	BALANCE	
					DEBIT	CREDIT

Name

PROBLEM 7.5A (continued)

GENERAL LEDGER

ACCOUNT ______ ACCOUNT NO. ______

DATE	DESCRIPTION	POST. REF.	DEBIT	CREDIT	BALANCE DEBIT	BALANCE CREDIT

ACCOUNT ______ ACCOUNT NO. ______

DATE	DESCRIPTION	POST. REF.	DEBIT	CREDIT	BALANCE DEBIT	BALANCE CREDIT

ACCOUNTS RECEIVABLE SUBSIDIARY LEDGER

NAME ______
ADDRESS ______

DATE	DESCRIPTION	POST. REF.	DEBIT	CREDIT	BALANCE

NAME ______
ADDRESS ______

DATE	DESCRIPTION	POST. REF.	DEBIT	CREDIT	BALANCE

Name

PROBLEM 7.5A (continued)

ACCOUNTS RECEIVABLE SUBSIDIARY LEDGER

NAME
ADDRESS

DATE		DESCRIPTION	POST. REF.	DEBIT	CREDIT	BALANCE

NAME
ADDRESS

DATE		DESCRIPTION	POST. REF.	DEBIT	CREDIT	BALANCE

NAME
ADDRESS

DATE		DESCRIPTION	POST. REF.	DEBIT	CREDIT	BALANCE

NAME
ADDRESS

DATE		DESCRIPTION	POST. REF.	DEBIT	CREDIT	BALANCE

Name

PROBLEM 7.5A (continued)

ACCOUNTS RECEIVABLE SUBSIDIARY LEDGER

NAME

ADDRESS

DATE		DESCRIPTION	POST. REF.	DEBIT	CREDIT	BALANCE

Compare the balance of the Accounts Receivable control account with the total of the schedule.

Analyze:

Name ____________________

PROBLEM 7.6A

GENERAL JOURNAL

PAGE ______

DATE	DESCRIPTION	POST. REF.	DEBIT	CREDIT

Name

PROBLEM 7.6A (continued)

GENERAL JOURNAL PAGE

	DATE		DESCRIPTION	POST. REF.	DEBIT	CREDIT	
1							1
2							2
3							3
4							4
5							5
6							6
7							7
8							8
9							9
10							10
11							11
12							12
13							13
14							14
15							15
16							16
17							17
18							18
19							19
20							20
21							21
22							22
23							23
24							24
25							25
26							26
27							27
28							28
29							29
30							30
31							31
32							32
33							33
34							34
35							35
36							36

Name

PROBLEM 7.6A (continued)

GENERAL LEDGER

ACCOUNT ______________________ ACCOUNT NO. ______

DATE		DESCRIPTION	POST. REF.	DEBIT	CREDIT	BALANCE DEBIT	BALANCE CREDIT

ACCOUNT ______________________ ACCOUNT NO. ______

DATE		DESCRIPTION	POST. REF.	DEBIT	CREDIT	BALANCE DEBIT	BALANCE CREDIT

ACCOUNT ______________________ ACCOUNT NO. ______

DATE		DESCRIPTION	POST. REF.	DEBIT	CREDIT	BALANCE DEBIT	BALANCE CREDIT

Name

PROBLEM 7.6A (continued)

GENERAL LEDGER

ACCOUNT ______ ACCOUNT NO. ______

DATE		DESCRIPTION	POST. REF.	DEBIT	CREDIT	BALANCE	
						DEBIT	CREDIT

ACCOUNT ______ ACCOUNT NO. ______

DATE		DESCRIPTION	POST. REF.	DEBIT	CREDIT	BALANCE	
						DEBIT	CREDIT

Analyze: ______

Name

PROBLEM 7.1B

GENERAL JOURNAL

PAGE

DATE		DESCRIPTION	POST. REF.	DEBIT	CREDIT

Name ______________________

PROBLEM 7.1B (continued)

GENERAL JOURNAL PAGE ______

	DATE		DESCRIPTION	POST. REF.	DEBIT	CREDIT	
1							1
2							2
3							3
4							4
5							5
6							6
7							7
8							8
9							9
10							10
11							11

GENERAL LEDGER

ACCOUNT ______________________ ACCOUNT NO. ______

DATE		DESCRIPTION	POST. REF.	DEBIT	CREDIT	BALANCE	
						DEBIT	CREDIT

ACCOUNT ______________________ ACCOUNT NO. ______

DATE		DESCRIPTION	POST. REF.	DEBIT	CREDIT	BALANCE	
						DEBIT	CREDIT

Name ____________________

PROBLEM 7.1B (continued)

ACCOUNT ____________________ ACCOUNT NO. ________

DATE	DESCRIPTION	POST. REF.	DEBIT	CREDIT	BALANCE DEBIT	BALANCE CREDIT

ACCOUNT ____________________ ACCOUNT NO. ________

DATE	DESCRIPTION	POST. REF.	DEBIT	CREDIT	BALANCE DEBIT	BALANCE CREDIT

Analyze: ____________________

Name

PROBLEM 7.2B

GENERAL JOURNAL

PAGE

DATE		DESCRIPTION	POST. REF.	DEBIT	CREDIT

Name

PROBLEM 7.2B (continued)

GENERAL JOURNAL

PAGE

DATE	DESCRIPTION	POST. REF.	DEBIT	CREDIT

Analyze:

Name ____________________

PROBLEM 7.3B

GENERAL LEDGER

ACCOUNT ____________________ ACCOUNT NO. ________

DATE	DESCRIPTION	POST. REF.	DEBIT	CREDIT	BALANCE	
					DEBIT	CREDIT

ACCOUNT ____________________ ACCOUNT NO. ________

DATE	DESCRIPTION	POST. REF.	DEBIT	CREDIT	BALANCE	
					DEBIT	CREDIT

Name ______________________________

PROBLEM 7.3B (continued)

ACCOUNT ______________________________ ACCOUNT NO. __________

DATE		DESCRIPTION	POST. REF.	DEBIT	CREDIT	BALANCE	
						DEBIT	CREDIT

ACCOUNT ______________________________ ACCOUNT NO. __________

DATE		DESCRIPTION	POST. REF.	DEBIT	CREDIT	BALANCE	
						DEBIT	CREDIT

ACCOUNT ______________________________ ACCOUNT NO. __________

DATE		DESCRIPTION	POST. REF.	DEBIT	CREDIT	BALANCE	
						DEBIT	CREDIT

Name

PROBLEM 7.3B (continued)

ACCOUNTS RECEIVABLE SUBSIDIARY LEDGER

NAME

ADDRESS

DATE		DESCRIPTION	POST. REF.	DEBIT	CREDIT	BALANCE

NAME

ADDRESS

DATE		DESCRIPTION	POST. REF.	DEBIT	CREDIT	BALANCE

NAME

ADDRESS

DATE		DESCRIPTION	POST. REF.	DEBIT	CREDIT	BALANCE

NAME

ADDRESS

DATE		DESCRIPTION	POST. REF.	DEBIT	CREDIT	BALANCE

Name

PROBLEM 7.3B (continued)

NAME

ADDRESS

DATE		DESCRIPTION	POST. REF.	DEBIT	CREDIT	BALANCE

Compare the balance of the Accounts Receivable control account with the total of the schedule.

Analyze:

Name ______________________

PROBLEM 7.4B

GENERAL JOURNAL

PAGE ______

DATE		DESCRIPTION	POST. REF.	DEBIT	CREDIT

Name ____________________

PROBLEM 7.4B (continued)

GENERAL JOURNAL PAGE ______

	DATE		DESCRIPTION	POST. REF.	DEBIT	CREDIT	
1							1
2							2
3							3
4							4
5							5
6							6
7							7
8							8
9							9
10							10
11							11
12							12
13							13
14							14
15							15
16							16
17							17
18							18
19							19
20							20
21							21
22							22
23							23
24							24
25							25
26							26
27							27
28							28
29							29
30							30
31							31
32							32
33							33
34							34
35							35
36							36
37							37

Name

PROBLEM 7.4B (continued)

GENERAL JOURNAL

PAGE

	DATE		DESCRIPTION	POST. REF.	DEBIT	CREDIT	
1							1
2							2
3							3
4							4
5							5
6							6
7							7
8							8
9							9
10							10
11							11
12							12
13							13
14							14
15							15

Analyze:

PROBLEM 7.5B

GENERAL LEDGER

ACCOUNT ACCOUNT NO.

DATE		DESCRIPTION	POST. REF.	DEBIT	CREDIT	BALANCE	
						DEBIT	CREDIT

Name

PROBLEM 7.5B (continued)

ACCOUNT ACCOUNT NO.

DATE		DESCRIPTION	POST. REF.	DEBIT	CREDIT	BALANCE DEBIT	BALANCE CREDIT

ACCOUNT ACCOUNT NO.

DATE		DESCRIPTION	POST. REF.	DEBIT	CREDIT	BALANCE DEBIT	BALANCE CREDIT

Name

PROBLEM 7.5B (continued)

ACCOUNT ______ ACCOUNT NO. ______

DATE		DESCRIPTION	POST. REF.	DEBIT	CREDIT	BALANCE	
						DEBIT	CREDIT

ACCOUNT ______ ACCOUNT NO. ______

DATE		DESCRIPTION	POST. REF.	DEBIT	CREDIT	BALANCE	
						DEBIT	CREDIT

ACCOUNTS RECEIVABLE SUBSIDIARY LEDGER

NAME ______

ADDRESS ______

DATE		DESCRIPTION	POST. REF.	DEBIT	CREDIT	BALANCE

NAME ______

ADDRESS ______

DATE		DESCRIPTION	POST. REF.	DEBIT	CREDIT	BALANCE

Name ______________________

PROBLEM 7.5B (continued)

NAME ______________________
ADDRESS ______________________

DATE		DESCRIPTION	POST. REF.	DEBIT	CREDIT	BALANCE

NAME ______________________
ADDRESS ______________________

DATE		DESCRIPTION	POST. REF.	DEBIT	CREDIT	BALANCE

NAME ______________________
ADDRESS ______________________

DATE		DESCRIPTION	POST. REF.	DEBIT	CREDIT	BALANCE

NAME ______________________
ADDRESS ______________________

DATE		DESCRIPTION	POST. REF.	DEBIT	CREDIT	BALANCE

Name

PROBLEM 7.5B (continued)

NAME
ADDRESS

DATE		DESCRIPTION	POST. REF.	DEBIT	CREDIT	BALANCE

Compare the balance of the Accounts Receivable control account with the total of the schedule.

Analyze:

Name

PROBLEM 7.6B

GENERAL JOURNAL

PAGE ______

DATE		DESCRIPTION	POST. REF.	DEBIT	CREDIT

Name

PROBLEM 7.6B (continued)

GENERAL JOURNAL

PAGE

DATE	DESCRIPTION	POST. REF.	DEBIT	CREDIT

Name ______________________

PROBLEM 7.6B (continued)

GENERAL LEDGER

ACCOUNT ______________________ ACCOUNT NO. ______

DATE	DESCRIPTION	POST. REF.	DEBIT	CREDIT	BALANCE DEBIT	BALANCE CREDIT

ACCOUNT ______________________ ACCOUNT NO. ______

DATE	DESCRIPTION	POST. REF.	DEBIT	CREDIT	BALANCE DEBIT	BALANCE CREDIT

ACCOUNT ______________________ ACCOUNT NO. ______

DATE	DESCRIPTION	POST. REF.	DEBIT	CREDIT	BALANCE DEBIT	BALANCE CREDIT

Name

PROBLEM 7.6B (continued)

ACCOUNT ______________________ ACCOUNT NO. ________

DATE		DESCRIPTION	POST. REF.	DEBIT	CREDIT	BALANCE	
						DEBIT	CREDIT

ACCOUNT ______________________ ACCOUNT NO. ________

DATE		DESCRIPTION	POST. REF.	DEBIT	CREDIT	BALANCE	
						DEBIT	CREDIT

Analyze: ____

Name

CRITICAL THINKING PROBLEM 7.1

GENERAL JOURNAL

PAGE

DATE	DESCRIPTION	POST. REF.	DEBIT	CREDIT

Name ____________________

CRITICAL THINKING PROBLEM 7.1 (continued)

GENERAL JOURNAL

PAGE ______

DATE		DESCRIPTION	POST. REF.	DEBIT	CREDIT

Name

CRITICAL THINKING PROBLEM 7.1 (continued)

ACCOUNT ______ ACCOUNT NO. ______

DATE		DESCRIPTION	POST. REF.	DEBIT	CREDIT	BALANCE DEBIT	BALANCE CREDIT

ACCOUNTS RECEIVABLE SUBSIDIARY LEDGER

NAME ______
ADDRESS ______

DATE		DESCRIPTION	POST. REF.	DEBIT	CREDIT	BALANCE

NAME ______
ADDRESS ______

DATE		DESCRIPTION	POST. REF.	DEBIT	CREDIT	BALANCE

Name

CRITICAL THINKING PROBLEM 7.1 (continued)

ACCOUNTS RECEIVABLE SUBSIDIARY LEDGER

NAME

ADDRESS

DATE		DESCRIPTION	POST. REF.	DEBIT	CREDIT	BALANCE

NAME

ADDRESS

DATE		DESCRIPTION	POST. REF.	DEBIT	CREDIT	BALANCE

NAME

ADDRESS

DATE		DESCRIPTION	POST. REF.	DEBIT	CREDIT	BALANCE

Name ______________________

CRITICAL THINKING PROBLEM 7.2

1. ______________________

2. ______________________

3. ______________________

4. ______________________

Chapter 7 Practice Test Answer Key

Part A True-False

1.	**T**	**11.**	**T**
2.	**T**	**12.**	**T**
3.	**T**	**13.**	**F**
4.	**F**	**14.**	**F**
5.	**F**	**15.**	**T**
6.	**F**	**16.**	**F**
7.	**F**	**17.**	**T**
8.	**F**	**18.**	**F**
9.	**T**	**19.**	**F**
10.	**T**	**20.**	**F**

Part B Matching

1. g
2. c
3. e
4. a
5. b
6. d
7. f

Part C Exercises

1. The balance was carried over from December 2015.
2. By referring to a copy of Sales Slip 101.
3. It was most likely a sales return or allowance. Refer to the January 17 entry on page 1 of the general journal.

Part D Exercise

GENERAL JOURNAL

PAGE 14

DATE		DESCRIPTION	POST. REF.	DEBIT	CREDIT
2016					
April	1	Accounts Receivable/Kisling's Kitchens		3500 00	
		Sales			3500 00
		Sold merchandise on account to			
		Kisling's Kitchens, Invoice 1001,			
		terms 2/10, n/30.			
	5	Sales returns and allowances		250 00	
		Accounts Receivable/Kisling's Kitchens			250 00
		Issued Credit Memorandum 102 to Kisling's			
		Kitchens for damaged merchandise			
	10	Sales Discounts (2% * ($3,500 − $250))		65 00	
		Cash ($3,250 − $65 discount)		3185 00	
		Accounts Receivable/Kisling's Kitchens			3250 00
		Received payment from Kisling's Kitchens for			
		Invoice 1001 dated April 1, less return on April 5.			

CHAPTER 8

Accounting for Purchases, Accounts Payable, and Cash Payments

STUDY GUIDE

Understanding the Chapter

Objectives

1. Record purchases of merchandise on credit in a general journal. **2.** Compute the net delivered cost of purchases. **3.** Post from the general journal to the general ledger accounts. **4.** Post transactions to the accounts payable subsidiary ledger. **5.** Prepare a schedule of accounts payable. **6.** Demonstrate knowledge of the procedures for effective internal control of purchases. **7.** Record purchases, sales, returns, cash payments and cash receipts using the perpetual inventory system. **8.** Define the accounting terms new to this chapter.

Reading Assignment

Read Chapter 8 in the textbook. Complete the textbook Section Self Review as you finish reading each section of the chapter, and the Comprehensive Self Review at the end of the chapter. Refer to the Chapter 8 Glossary or to the Glossary at the end of the book to find definitions for terms that are not familiar to you.

Activities

❑ **Thinking Critically** — Answer the *Thinking Critically* questions for Williams-Sonoma and Managerial Implications.

❑ **Discussion Questions** — Answer each assigned discussion question in Chapter 8.

❑ **Exercises** — Complete each assigned exercise in Chapter 8. Use the forms provided in this SGWP. The objectives covered by an exercise are given after the exercise number. If you need help with an exercise, review the portion of the chapter related to the objective(s) covered.

❑ **Problems A/B** — Complete each assigned problem in Chapter 8. Use the forms provided in this SGWP. The objectives covered by a problem are given after the problem number. If you need help with a problem, review the portion of the chapter related to the objective(s) covered.

❑ **Critical Thinking Problems** — Complete the critical thinking problems as assigned. Use the forms provided in this SGWP.

❑ **Business Connections** — Complete the Business Connections activities as assigned to gain a deeper understanding of Chapter 8 concepts.

Practice Tests

Complete the Practice Tests, which cover the main points in your reading assignment. Compare your answers with those in the Practice Test Answer Key for Chapter 8 at the end of this chapter. If you have answered any questions incorrectly, review the related section of the text.

Part A True-False *For each of the following statements, circle T in the answer column if the statement is true or F if the statement is false.*

T F **1.** The journal entry to record purchases of merchandise on account requires a credit to **Accounts Payable**.

T F **2.** Prenumbered forms should be used for purchase requisitions, purchase orders, and checks.

T F **3.** Purchases discounts and purchases returns effectively increase a company's cost of purchases.

T F **4.** Freight charges on merchandise inventory purchased FOB Shipping Point should be debited to the **Purchases** account.

T F **5.** The accounting department should check the quantities, prices, and math on all invoices from suppliers before the purchase is recorded in the general journal.

T F **6.** **Purchases Returns and Allowances** has a normal credit balance.

T F **7.** **Purchases Discounts** has a normal debit balance.

T F **8.** The individual in charge of authorizing purchases of merchandise should also write the check in payment of those purchases.

T F **9.** The purchase order should specify the exact items, cost, quantity, and credit terms of the order.

T F **10.** Merchandise purchased has a list price of $4,000, and is subject to a trade discount of 30 percent. The credit terms are 1/10, n/30. The amount of payment if made within 10 days of the invoice date is $2,772.

T F **11.** Merchandise costing $2,500 FOB shipping point, 1/10, n/30, was purchased April 1 on account. Freight costs of $130 were prepaid by the vendor and added to the invoice. If the bill is paid within ten days, the amount of the purchase discount is $26.30.

T F **12.** The entry to record the return of merchandise from the buyer to the seller is debit **Accounts Payable**, credit **Purchases**.

T F **13.** Net purchases equals **Purchases** less **Purchases Returns and Allowances** plus Purchases **Discounts**.

T F **14.** **Freight In** becomes part of the delivered cost of purchases shown in the income statement.

T F **15.** **Purchases Returns and Allowances** is a contra-revenue account.

T F **16.** After a payment on account to a vendor is recorded in the general journal, it should be posted to both the general ledger and the vendor's account in the accounts payable subsidiary ledger.

T F **17.** After all postings are completed, the total of the individual balances in the accounts payable subsidiary ledger should be equal to the balance of the **Accounts Receivable** control account in the general ledger.

T F **18.** The balance of each creditor's account in the accounts payable subsidiary ledger is not computed until the end of the month.

T F **19.** A receiving report is prepared to show the quantity of goods received and their condition.

T F **20.** Purchases of merchandise inventory are debited to the **Purchases** account when the periodic system is used, and to the Merchandise Inventory account when the perpetual system is used.

Part B Exercise *For each of the following situations, calculate the amount that should be paid at the due date of the invoice. All purchases were made FOB Shipping Point.*

	1	2	3	4	5
Invoice Date	March 11	April 1	May 15	June 10	July 2
Date Paid	March 31	April 10	May 24	June 20	July 12
Purchase	$1,200	$2,500	$3,500	$3,000	$3,400
Credit Terms	1/10, n/30	1/10, n/30	n/30	2/10, n/30	1/10, n/30
Freight added to invoice	–	–	$100	$200	$150
Returns	–	–	–	–	$200

Demonstration Problem

L'Amour Cosmetics is a cosmetics wholesaler that commenced business on September 1, 2016. L'Amour Cosmetics purchases merchandise for cash and on open account. L'Amour Cosmetics uses the periodic system. In September 2016, L'Amour Cosmetics engaged in the following purchasing and cash payment activities.

DATE	TRANSACTIONS
2016	
Sept. 1	Issued Check 101 to purchase merchandise, $3,500.
3	Purchased merchandise for $1,300 from Bella Skin Products, Invoice 506, terms 1/10, n/30.
5	Purchased merchandise for $4,750, plus a freight charge of $100 from Gina's Cosmetics, Inc., Invoice 1100, terms 2/10, n/30.
9	Paid amount due to Bella Skin Products for purchase of September 3, less discount, Check 102.
10	Received Credit Memorandum 227 from Gina's Cosmetics, Inc. for damaged merchandise totaling $200 that was returned; the goods were purchased on Invoice 1100, dated September 5.
11	Purchased merchandise for $1,380 from Bella Skin Products, Invoice 512, terms 1/10, n/30.
14	Paid amount due to Gina's Cosmetics, Inc. for Invoice 1100 of September 5, less the return of September 10 and less the cash discount, check 103.
15	Purchased merchandise with a list price of $9,000 and trade discounts of 25% and 10% from Nutri-Skin Products, Invoice 1029, terms n/30.
20	Issued Check 104 to purchase merchandise, $2,400.
25	Returned merchandise purchased on September 20 as defective, receiving a cash refund of $230.
30	Purchased merchandise for $4,625, plus a freight charge of $75 from Gina's Cosmetics, Inc., Invoice 1144, terms 2/10, n/30.

Instructions

1. Open the general ledger accounts and accounts payable subsidiary ledger accounts indicated below. Enter the balances as of September 1, 2016.
2. Journalize the transactions above in a general journal. Start the journal with page 10.
3. Post the transactions to the appropriate accounts in the general ledger and the Accounts Payable subsidiary ledger.
4. Prepare a schedule of accounts payable at September 30, 2016.

Genral Ledger Accounts

101 Cash, $31,200 Dr.
201 Accounts Payable
501 Purchases
502 Purchases Returns and Allowances
503 Purchases Discounts
504 Freight In

Accounts Payable Subsidiary Ledger Accounts

Bella Skin Products
Gina's Cosmetics, Inc.
Nutri-Skin Products

SOLUTION

GENERAL JOURNAL PAGE 10

DATE		DESCRIPTION	POST. REF.	DEBIT	CREDIT
2016					
Sept.	1	Purchases	501	3500 00	
		Cash	101		3500 00
		Purchased merchandise, Check 101			
	3	Purchases	501	1300 00	
		Accounts Payable/Bella Skin Products	201 ✓		1300 00
		Purchased merchandise on account,			
		Invoice 506, terms 1/10, n/30			
	5	Purchases	501	4750 00	
		Freight In	504	100 00	
		Accounts Payable/Gina's Cosmetics, Inc.	201 ✓		4850 00
		Purchased merchandise on account,			
		Invoice 1100, terms 2/10, n/30			
	9	Accounts Payable/Bella Skin Products	201 ✓	1300 00	
		Purchases Discounts ($1,300 × 1%)	503		13 00
		Cash ($1,300 − $13)	101		1287 00
		Paid amount due on Invoice 506,			
		Check 102			
	10	Accounts Payable/Gina's Cosmetics, Inc.	201 ✓	200 00	
		Purchases Returns and Allowances	502		200 00
		Received Credit Memorandum 227 for return			
		of damaged merchandise			
	11	Purchases	501	1380 00	
		Accounts Payable/Bella Skin Products	201 ✓		1380 00
		Purchased merchandise on account,			
		Invoice 512, terms 1/10, n/30			
	14	Accounts Payable/Gina's Cosmetics, Inc. ($4,850 − 200)	201 ✓	4650 00	
		Purchases Discounts ($4,550 × 2%)	503		91 00
		Cash	101		4559 00
		Paid amount owed on Invoice 1100,			
		Check 103			

SOLUTION (continued)

GENERAL JOURNAL

PAGE 11

DATE		DESCRIPTION	POST. REF.	DEBIT	CREDIT
2016					
Sept.	15	Purchases ($9,000 − $2,250 = $6,750; $6,750 − $675 = $6,075)	501	6,075.00	
		Accounts Payable/Nutri-Skin Products	201 ✓		6,075.00
		Purchased merchandise on account,			
		Invoice 1029, terms n/30			
	20	Purchases	501	2,400.00	
		Cash	101		2,400.00
		Purchased merchandise, Check 104			
	25	Cash	101	230.00	
		Purchases Returns and Allowances	502		230.00
		Received cash for return of defective merchandise			
		purchased September 20			
	30	Purchases	501	4,625.00	
		Freight In	504	75.00	
		Accounts Payable/Gina's Cosmetics, Inc.	201 ✓		4,700.00
		Purchased merchandise on account,			
		Invoice 1144, terms 2/10, n/30			

GENERAL LEDGER

ACCOUNT Cash ACCOUNT NO. 101

DATE		DESCRIPTION	POST. REF.	DEBIT	CREDIT	BALANCE DEBIT	BALANCE CREDIT
2016							
Sept.	1	Balance	✓			31,200.00	
	1		J10		3,500.00	27,700.00	
	9		J10		1,287.00	26,413.00	
	14		J10		4,559.00	21,854.00	
	20		J11		2,400.00	19,454.00	
	25		J11	230.00		19,684.00	

SOLUTION (continued)

ACCOUNT **Accounts Payable** ACCOUNT NO. **201**

DATE		DESCRIPTION	POST. REF.	DEBIT	CREDIT	BALANCE DEBIT	BALANCE CREDIT
2016							
Sept.	**3**		**J10**		**1,300.00**		**1,300.00**
	5		**J10**		**4,850.00**		**6,150.00**
	9		**J10**	**1,300.00**			**4,850.00**
	10		**J10**	**200.00**			**4,650.00**
	11		**J10**		**1,380.00**		**6,030.00**
	14		**J10**	**4,650.00**			**1,380.00**
	15		**J11**		**6,075.00**		**7,455.00**
	30		**J11**		**4,700.00**		**12,155.00**

ACCOUNT **Purchases** ACCOUNT NO. **501**

DATE		DESCRIPTION	POST. REF.	DEBIT	CREDIT	BALANCE DEBIT	BALANCE CREDIT
2016							
Sept.	**1**		**J10**	**3,500.00**		**3,500.00**	
	3		**J10**	**1,300.00**		**4,800.00**	
	5		**J10**	**4,750.00**		**9,550.00**	
	11		**J10**	**1,380.00**		**10,930.00**	
	15		**J11**	**6,075.00**		**17,005.00**	
	20		**J11**	**2,400.00**		**19,405.00**	
	30		**J11**	**4,625.00**		**24,030.00**	

ACCOUNT **Purchases Returns and Allowances** ACCOUNT NO. **502**

DATE		DESCRIPTION	POST. REF.	DEBIT	CREDIT	BALANCE DEBIT	BALANCE CREDIT
2016							
Sept.	**10**		**J10**		**200.00**		**200.00**
	25		**J11**		**230.00**		**430.00**

SOLUTION (continued)

ACCOUNT **Purchases Discounts** ACCOUNT NO. **503**

DATE		DESCRIPTION	POST. REF.	DEBIT	CREDIT	BALANCE DEBIT	BALANCE CREDIT
2016							
Sept.	**9**		**J10**		**13 00**		**13 00**
	14		**J10**		**91 00**		**104 00**

ACCOUNT **Freight In** ACCOUNT NO. **504**

DATE		DESCRIPTION	POST. REF.	DEBIT	CREDIT	BALANCE DEBIT	BALANCE CREDIT
2016							
Sept.	**5**		**J10**	**100 00**		**100 00**	
	30		**J11**	**75 00**		**175 00**	

ACCOUNTS PAYABLE SUBSIDIARY LEDGER

NAME **Bella Skin Products** TERMS **1/10, n/30**

ADDRESS

DATE		DESCRIPTION	POST. REF.	DEBIT	CREDIT	BALANCE
2016						
Sept.	**3**	**Invoice 506**	**J10**		**1300 00**	**1300 00**
	9		**J10**	**1300 00**		**-0-**
	11	**Invoice 512**	**J10**		**1380 00**	**1380 00**

NAME **Gina's Cosmetics, Inc.** TERMS **2/10, n/30**

ADDRESS

DATE		DESCRIPTION	POST. REF.	DEBIT	CREDIT	BALANCE
2016						
Sept.	**5**	**Invoice 1100**	**J10**		**4850 00**	**4850 00**
	10	**CM 227**	**J10**	**200 00**		**4650 00**
	14		**J10**	**4650 00**		**-0-**
	30	**Invoice 1144**	**J11**		**4700 00**	**4700 00**

SOLUTION (continued)

NAME Nutri-Skin Products TERMS n/30

ADDRESS

DATE		DESCRIPTION	POST. REF.	DEBIT	CREDIT	BALANCE
2016						
Sept.	15	Invoice 1029	J11		6,075.00	6,075.00

L'Amour Cosmetics
Schedule of Accounts Payable
September 30, 2016

Bella Skin Products	1,380.00
Gina's Cosmetics, Inc.	4,700.00
Nutri-Skin Products	6,075.00
Total	12,155.00

WORKING PAPERS

Name ______________________________

EXERCISE 8.1

_____ Purchases

_____ Purchases Returns and Allowances

_____ Purchases Discounts

_____ Freight In

EXERCISE 8.2

GENERAL JOURNAL

PAGE _____

	DATE		DESCRIPTION	POST. REF.	DEBIT	CREDIT	
1							1
2							2
3							3
4							4
5							5
6							6
7							7
8							8
9							9
10							10
11							11
12							12
13							13
14							14
15							15
16							16
17							17
18							18
19							19
20							20
21							21
22							22
23							23
24							24
25							25
26							26
27							27

Name ______________________

EXERCISE 8.3

GENERAL JOURNAL

PAGE ______

DATE		DESCRIPTION	POST. REF.	DEBIT	CREDIT

Name ______________________

EXERCISE 8.4

GENERAL JOURNAL PAGE ______

DATE	DESCRIPTION	POST. REF.	DEBIT	CREDIT

Name

EXERCISE 8.5

GENERAL JOURNAL PAGE

DATE		DESCRIPTION	POST. REF.	DEBIT	CREDIT

EXERCISE 8.6

Bryant Company

GENERAL JOURNAL PAGE

DATE		DESCRIPTION	POST. REF.	DEBIT	CREDIT

Name ____________________

EXERCISE 8.6 (continued)

Schmidt, Inc.

GENERAL JOURNAL PAGE ____

DATE		DESCRIPTION	POST. REF.	DEBIT	CREDIT

Name ____________________

EXERCISE 8.7

EXERCISE 8.8

GENERAL JOURNAL — PAGE 40

	DATE		DESCRIPTION	POST. REF.	DEBIT	CREDIT	
1	2013						1
2	Jan.	8	Accounts Payable/Stamos Distributors		200 00		2
3			Cash			200 00	3
4			Made partial payment on account, check 1240				4
5							5
6		10	Accounts Payable/Evans Enterprises		100 00		6
7			Purchases Returns and Allowances			100 00	7
8			Received Credit memorandum 123 as allowance				8
9			for discolored merchandise				9
10							10
11							11
12							12
13							13
14							14

Name

EXERCISE 8.8 (continued)

ACCOUNT **Accounts Payable** ACCOUNT NO. **202**

DATE		DESCRIPTION	POST. REF.	DEBIT	CREDIT	BALANCE DEBIT	BALANCE CREDIT
2013							
Jan.	**1**	**Balance**	✔				**5,100.00**

NAME **Evans Enterprises** TERMS

ADDRESS

DATE		DESCRIPTION	POST. REF.	DEBIT	CREDIT	BALANCE
2013						
Jan.	**1**	**Balance**	✔			**1,100.00**

NAME **Stamos Distributors** TERMS

ADDRESS

DATE		DESCRIPTION	POST. REF.	DEBIT	CREDIT	BALANCE
2013						
Jan.	**1**	**Balance**	✔			**2,600.00**

NAME **Tonetta Company** TERMS

ADDRESS

DATE		DESCRIPTION	POST. REF.	DEBIT	CREDIT	BALANCE
2013						
Jan.	**1**	**Balance**	✔			**1,400.00**

Name

EXERCISE 8.9

2. Does the total of your accounts payable schedule agree with the balance of the accounts payable account in the general ledger at January 31, 2013?

Name

PROBLEM 8.1A

GENERAL JOURNAL

PAGE

DATE		DESCRIPTION	POST. REF.	DEBIT	CREDIT

Name ______________________

PROBLEM 8.1A (continued)

GENERAL LEDGER

ACCOUNT ______________________ ACCOUNT NO. ______

DATE		DESCRIPTION	POST. REF.	DEBIT	CREDIT	BALANCE DEBIT	BALANCE CREDIT

ACCOUNT ______________________ ACCOUNT NO. ______

DATE		DESCRIPTION	POST. REF.	DEBIT	CREDIT	BALANCE DEBIT	BALANCE CREDIT

ACCOUNT ______________________ ACCOUNT NO. ______

DATE		DESCRIPTION	POST. REF.	DEBIT	CREDIT	BALANCE DEBIT	BALANCE CREDIT

Name

PROBLEM 8.1A (continued)

ACCOUNT ______________________ ACCOUNT NO. ________

DATE		DESCRIPTION	POST. REF.	DEBIT	CREDIT	BALANCE DEBIT	BALANCE CREDIT

Analyze: ______________________

Name

PROBLEM 8.2A

GENERAL JOURNAL PAGE

DATE	DESCRIPTION	POST. REF.	DEBIT	CREDIT

Name

PROBLEM 8.2A (continued)

GENERAL JOURNAL

PAGE

	DATE	DESCRIPTION	POST. REF.	DEBIT	CREDIT	
1						1
2						2
3						3
4						4
5						5
6						6
7						7
8						8
9						9
10						10
11						11
12						12
13						13
14						14
15						15
16						16
17						17
18						18
19						19
20						20
21						21
22						22
23						23
24						24
25						25

Analyze:

PROBLEM 8.3A

GENERAL LEDGER

ACCOUNT ACCOUNT NO.

DATE	DESCRIPTION	POST. REF.	DEBIT	CREDIT	BALANCE	
					DEBIT	CREDIT

Name

PROBLEM 8.3A (continued)

ACCOUNT ACCOUNT NO.

DATE		DESCRIPTION	POST. REF.	DEBIT	CREDIT	BALANCE DEBIT	BALANCE CREDIT

ACCOUNT ACCOUNT NO.

DATE		DESCRIPTION	POST. REF.	DEBIT	CREDIT	BALANCE DEBIT	BALANCE CREDIT

ACCOUNT ACCOUNT NO.

DATE		DESCRIPTION	POST. REF.	DEBIT	CREDIT	BALANCE DEBIT	BALANCE CREDIT

Name

PROBLEM 8.3A (continued)

ACCOUNT ACCOUNT NO.

DATE		DESCRIPTION	POST. REF.	DEBIT	CREDIT	BALANCE DEBIT	BALANCE CREDIT

ACCOUNT ACCOUNT NO.

DATE		DESCRIPTION	POST. REF.	DEBIT	CREDIT	BALANCE DEBIT	BALANCE CREDIT

ACCOUNTS PAYABLE SUBSIDIARY LEDGER

NAME TERMS
ADDRESS

DATE		DESCRIPTION	POST. REF.	DEBIT	CREDIT	BALANCE

NAME TERMS
ADDRESS

DATE		DESCRIPTION	POST. REF.	DEBIT	CREDIT	BALANCE

Name ______________________

PROBLEM 8.3A (continued)

NAME ______________________ TERMS ______
ADDRESS ______________________

DATE		DESCRIPTION	POST. REF.	DEBIT	CREDIT	BALANCE

NAME ______________________ TERMS ______
ADDRESS ______________________

DATE		DESCRIPTION	POST. REF.	DEBIT	CREDIT	BALANCE

Compare the balance of the Accounts Payable control account with the total of the schedule.

Analyze:

Name

PROBLEM 8.4A

GENERAL JOURNAL

PAGE

DATE	DESCRIPTION	POST. REF.	DEBIT	CREDIT

Name ______________________

PROBLEM 8.4A (continued)

GENERAL JOURNAL PAGE ______

DATE	DESCRIPTION	POST. REF.	DEBIT	CREDIT

Analyze: ______________________

Name

PROBLEM 8.5A

GENERAL LEDGER

ACCOUNT ______ ACCOUNT NO. ______

DATE		DESCRIPTION	POST. REF.	DEBIT	CREDIT	BALANCE	
						DEBIT	CREDIT

ACCOUNT ______ ACCOUNT NO. ______

DATE		DESCRIPTION	POST. REF.	DEBIT	CREDIT	BALANCE	
						DEBIT	CREDIT

ACCOUNT ______ ACCOUNT NO. ______

DATE		DESCRIPTION	POST. REF.	DEBIT	CREDIT	BALANCE	
						DEBIT	CREDIT

Name

PROBLEM 8.5A (continued)

ACCOUNT ______ ACCOUNT NO. ______

DATE		DESCRIPTION	POST. REF.	DEBIT	CREDIT	BALANCE DEBIT	BALANCE CREDIT

ACCOUNT ______ ACCOUNT NO. ______

DATE		DESCRIPTION	POST. REF.	DEBIT	CREDIT	BALANCE DEBIT	BALANCE CREDIT

ACCOUNT ______ ACCOUNT NO. ______

DATE		DESCRIPTION	POST. REF.	DEBIT	CREDIT	BALANCE DEBIT	BALANCE CREDIT

ACCOUNTS PAYABLE SUBSIDIARY LEDGER

NAME ______ TERMS ______

ADDRESS ______

DATE		DESCRIPTION	POST. REF.	DEBIT	CREDIT	BALANCE

Name ______________________

PROBLEM 8.5A (continued)

NAME ______________________ TERMS ______

ADDRESS ______________________

DATE		DESCRIPTION	POST. REF.	DEBIT	CREDIT	BALANCE

NAME ______________________ TERMS ______

ADDRESS ______________________

DATE		DESCRIPTION	POST. REF.	DEBIT	CREDIT	BALANCE

Analyze: ______________________

Name ______________________

PROBLEM 8.6A

Brown Company

GENERAL JOURNAL

PAGE ______

DATE	DESCRIPTION	POST. REF.	DEBIT	CREDIT

Name

PROBLEM 8.6A (continued)

Smith, Inc.

GENERAL JOURNAL

PAGE

DATE	DESCRIPTION	POST. REF.	DEBIT	CREDIT

PROBLEM 8.6A (continued)

GENERAL LEDGER – Brown Company

ACCOUNT ACCOUNT NO.

DATE		DESCRIPTION	POST. REF.	DEBIT	CREDIT	BALANCE DEBIT	BALANCE CREDIT

ACCOUNTS PAYABLE SUBSIDIARY LEDGER – Brown Company

NAME TERMS

ADDRESS

DATE		DESCRIPTION	POST. REF.	DEBIT	CREDIT	BALANCE

Name ____________________

PROBLEM 8.6A (continued)

GENERAL LEDGER – Smith, Inc.

ACCOUNT ____________________ ACCOUNT NO. ________

DATE		DESCRIPTION	POST. REF.	DEBIT	CREDIT	BALANCE	
						DEBIT	CREDIT

ACCOUNTS RECEIVABLE SUBSIDIARY LEDGER – Smith, Inc.

NAME ____________________

ADDRESS ____________________

DATE		DESCRIPTION	POST. REF.	DEBIT	CREDIT	BALANCE

Analyze: ____________________

Name

PROBLEM 8.1B

GENERAL JOURNAL

PAGE

DATE		DESCRIPTION	POST. REF.	DEBIT	CREDIT

Name ______________________

PROBLEM 8.1B (continued)

GENERAL LEDGER

ACCOUNT ______________________ ACCOUNT NO. ______

DATE		DESCRIPTION	POST. REF.	DEBIT	CREDIT	BALANCE	
						DEBIT	CREDIT

ACCOUNT ______________________ ACCOUNT NO. ______

DATE		DESCRIPTION	POST. REF.	DEBIT	CREDIT	BALANCE	
						DEBIT	CREDIT

ACCOUNT ______________________ ACCOUNT NO. ______

DATE		DESCRIPTION	POST. REF.	DEBIT	CREDIT	BALANCE	
						DEBIT	CREDIT

Name

PROBLEM 8.1B (continued)

ACCOUNT ______ ACCOUNT NO. ______

DATE		DESCRIPTION	POST. REF.	DEBIT	CREDIT	BALANCE DEBIT	BALANCE CREDIT

Analyze:

Name

PROBLEM 8.2B

GENERAL JOURNAL PAGE

DATE		DESCRIPTION	POST. REF.	DEBIT	CREDIT

Name ____________________

PROBLEM 8.2B (continued)

GENERAL JOURNAL PAGE ______

	DATE	DESCRIPTION	POST. REF.	DEBIT	CREDIT	
1						1
2						2
3						3
4						4
5						5
6						6
7						7
8						8
9						9
10						10
11						11
12						12
13						13
14						14
15						15
16						16
17						17
18						18
19						19
20						20
21						21
22						22
23						23

Analyze: ____________________

PROBLEM 8.3B

GENERAL LEDGER

ACCOUNT ____________________ ACCOUNT NO. ______

DATE	DESCRIPTION	POST. REF.	DEBIT	CREDIT	BALANCE	
					DEBIT	CREDIT

Name

PROBLEM 8.3B (continued)

ACCOUNT ______________________ ACCOUNT NO. ________

DATE		DESCRIPTION	POST. REF.	DEBIT	CREDIT	BALANCE	
						DEBIT	CREDIT

ACCOUNT ______________________ ACCOUNT NO. ________

DATE		DESCRIPTION	POST. REF.	DEBIT	CREDIT	BALANCE	
						DEBIT	CREDIT

ACCOUNT ______________________ ACCOUNT NO. ________

DATE		DESCRIPTION	POST. REF.	DEBIT	CREDIT	BALANCE	
						DEBIT	CREDIT

Name ____________________

PROBLEM 8.3B (continued)

ACCOUNT ____________________ ACCOUNT NO. ________

DATE		DESCRIPTION	POST. REF.	DEBIT	CREDIT	BALANCE	
						DEBIT	CREDIT

ACCOUNT ____________________ ACCOUNT NO. ________

DATE		DESCRIPTION	POST. REF.	DEBIT	CREDIT	BALANCE	
						DEBIT	CREDIT

ACCOUNTS PAYABLE SUBSIDIARY LEDGER

NAME ____________________ TERMS ________

ADDRESS ____________________

DATE		DESCRIPTION	POST. REF.	DEBIT	CREDIT	BALANCE

NAME ____________________ TERMS ________

ADDRESS ____________________

DATE		DESCRIPTION	POST. REF.	DEBIT	CREDIT	BALANCE

Name

PROBLEM 8.3B (continued)

NAME ______ TERMS ______
ADDRESS ______

DATE		DESCRIPTION	POST. REF.	DEBIT	CREDIT	BALANCE

NAME ______ TERMS ______
ADDRESS ______

DATE		DESCRIPTION	POST. REF.	DEBIT	CREDIT	BALANCE

Compare the balance of the Accounts Payable control account with the total of the schedule.

Analyze:

Name ______________________

PROBLEM 8.4B

GENERAL JOURNAL PAGE ______

DATE	DESCRIPTION	POST. REF.	DEBIT	CREDIT

Name ______________________________

PROBLEM 8.4B (continued)

GENERAL JOURNAL — PAGE ______

	DATE		DESCRIPTION	POST. REF.	DEBIT	CREDIT	
1							1
2							2
3							3
4							4
5							5
6							6
7							7
8							8
9							9
10							10
11							11
12							12
13							13
14							14
15							15
16							16
17							17
18							18
19							19
20							20
21							21
22							22
23							23
24							24
25							25
26							26
27							27
28							28
29							29
30							30
31							31
32							32
33							33

Analyze: ______________________________

Name

PROBLEM 8.5B

GENERAL LEDGER

ACCOUNT ______________________ ACCOUNT NO. ______

DATE		DESCRIPTION	POST. REF.	DEBIT	CREDIT	BALANCE DEBIT	BALANCE CREDIT

ACCOUNT ______________________ ACCOUNT NO. ______

DATE		DESCRIPTION	POST. REF.	DEBIT	CREDIT	BALANCE DEBIT	BALANCE CREDIT

ACCOUNT ______________________ ACCOUNT NO. ______

DATE		DESCRIPTION	POST. REF.	DEBIT	CREDIT	BALANCE DEBIT	BALANCE CREDIT

Name ______________________

PROBLEM 8.5B (continued)

ACCOUNT ______________________ ACCOUNT NO. ________

DATE	DESCRIPTION	POST. REF.	DEBIT	CREDIT	BALANCE DEBIT	BALANCE CREDIT

ACCOUNT ______________________ ACCOUNT NO. ________

DATE	DESCRIPTION	POST. REF.	DEBIT	CREDIT	BALANCE DEBIT	BALANCE CREDIT

ACCOUNT ______________________ ACCOUNT NO. ________

DATE	DESCRIPTION	POST. REF.	DEBIT	CREDIT	BALANCE DEBIT	BALANCE CREDIT

ACCOUNTS PAYABLE SUBSIDIARY LEDGER

NAME ______________________ TERMS ________

ADDRESS ______________________

DATE	DESCRIPTION	POST. REF.	DEBIT	CREDIT	BALANCE

Name

PROBLEM 8.5B (continued)

NAME TERMS
ADDRESS

DATE		DESCRIPTION	POST. REF.	DEBIT	CREDIT	BALANCE

NAME TERMS
ADDRESS

DATE		DESCRIPTION	POST. REF.	DEBIT	CREDIT	BALANCE

Analyze:

Name

PROBLEM 8.6B

Banh Company

GENERAL JOURNAL

PAGE

DATE	DESCRIPTION	POST. REF.	DEBIT	CREDIT

Name ____________________

PROBLEM 8.6B (continued)

Santoni, Inc.

GENERAL JOURNAL

PAGE ____

DATE		DESCRIPTION	POST. REF.	DEBIT	CREDIT

Name ____________________

PROBLEM 8.6B (continued)

GENERAL JOURNAL – Banh Company

ACCOUNT ____________________ ACCOUNT NO. ________

DATE		DESCRIPTION	POST. REF.	DEBIT	CREDIT	BALANCE	
						DEBIT	CREDIT

ACCOUNTS PAYABLE SUBSIDIARY LEDGER – Banh Company

NAME ____________________ TERMS ________

ADDRESS ____________________

DATE		DESCRIPTION	POST. REF.	DEBIT	CREDIT	BALANCE

Name ______________________

PROBLEM 8.6B (continued)

GENERAL LEDGER – Santoni, Inc.

ACCOUNT ______________________ ACCOUNT NO. ________

DATE		DESCRIPTION	POST. REF.	DEBIT	CREDIT	BALANCE DEBIT	BALANCE CREDIT

ACCOUNTS RECEIVABLE SUBSIDIARY LEDGER – Santoni, Inc.

NAME ______________________

ADDRESS ______________________

DATE		DESCRIPTION	POST. REF.	DEBIT	CREDIT	BALANCE

Analyze: ______________________

Name ____________________

CRITICAL THINKING PROBLEM 8.1

GENERAL JOURNAL — PAGE ____

DATE		DESCRIPTION	POST. REF.	DEBIT	CREDIT

Name ____________________

CRITICAL THINKING PROBLEM 8.1 (continued)

GENERAL JOURNAL

PAGE ______

DATE		DESCRIPTION	POST. REF.	DEBIT	CREDIT

Name ____________________

CRITICAL THINKING PROBLEM 8.1 (continued)

GENERAL JOURNAL PAGE ______

DATE		DESCRIPTION	POST. REF.	DEBIT	CREDIT

Name

CRITICAL THINKING PROBLEM 8.2

1.

2.

Chapter 8 Practice Test Answer Key

Part A True-False	
1. T	**11. F**
2. T	**12. F**
3. F	**13. F**
4. F	**14. T**
5. T	**15. F**
6. T	**16. T**
7. F	**17. F**
8. F	**18. F**
9. T	**19. T**
10. T	**20. T**

Part B Exercises

1. $1,200.00; 2. $2,475.00; 3. $3,600.00; 4. $3,140.00; 5. $3,318.00. See details below.

	1	2	3	4	5
Original purchase	$1,200.00	$2,500.00	$3,500.00	$3,000.00	$3,400.00
Less returns	–	–	–	–	200.00
Subtotal	1,200.00	2,500.00	3,500.00	3,000.00	3,200.00
Less discount	–	25.00	–	60.00	32.00
Subtotal	1,200.00	2,475.00	3,500.00	2,940.00	3,168.00
Add freight	–	–	100.00	200.00	150.00
Amount due	$1,200.00	$2,475.00	$3,600.00	$3,140.00	$3,318.00

CHAPTER 9

Cash

STUDY GUIDE

Understanding the Chapter

Objectives

1. Account for cash short or over. **2.** Demonstrate a knowledge of procedures for a petty cash fund. **3.** Demonstrate a knowledge of internal control routines for cash. **4.** Write a check, endorse checks, prepare a bank deposit slip, and maintain a checkbook balance. **5.** Reconcile the monthly bank statement. **6.** Record any adjusting entries required from the bank reconciliation. **7.** Understand how businesses use online banking to manage cash activities. **8.** Define accounting terms new to this chapter.

Reading Assignment

Read Chapter 9 in the textbook. Complete the Section Self Review as you finish reading each section of the chapter, and the Comprehensive Self Review at the end of the chapter. Refer to the Chapter 9 Glossary or to the Glossary at the end of the book to find definitions for terms that are not familiar to you.

Activities

- ❑ **Thinking Critically** — Answer the *Thinking Critically* questions for CLIF Bars.
- ❑ **Discussion Questions** — Answer each assigned review question in Chapter 9.
- ❑ **Exercises** — Complete each assigned exercise in Chapter 9. Use the forms provided in this SGWP. The objectives covered by an exercise are given after the exercise number. If you need help with an exercise, review the portion of the chapter related to the objective(s) covered.
- ❑ **Problems A/B** — Complete each assigned problem in Chapter 9. Use the forms provided in this SGWP. The objectives covered by a problem are given after the problem number. If you need help with a problem, review the portion of the chapter related to the objective(s) covered.
- ❑ **Critical Thinking Problems** — Complete the critical thinking problems as assigned. Use the forms provided in this SGWP.
- ❑ **Business Connections** — Complete the Business Connections activities as assigned to gain a deeper understanding of Chapter 9 concepts.

Practice Tests

Complete the Practice Tests, which cover the main points in your reading assignment. Compare your answers with those in the Practice Test Answer Key for Chapter 9 at the end of this chapter. If you have answered any questions incorrectly, review the related section of the text.

Part A True-False *For each of the following statements, circle T in the answer column if the statement is true or F if the statement is false.*

T F **1.** The best form of endorsement for business purposes is the restrictive endorsement, which limits the use of the check to a stated purpose.

T F **2.** **Cash Short or Over** is a general ledger account that normally has a credit balance because cash tends to be short more often than over.

T F **3.** Internal controls are not necessary if payments are made by check.

T F **4.** The **Sales Tax Payable** account represents an expense of the business.

T F **5.** Except for petty cash payments, all payments should be made by check.

T F **6.** Correct internal control procedures require that the approval for paying all bills, writing all checks, and signing all checks should be the responsibility of the same person.

T F **7.** Cash received by mail should be deposited by the same person who accepts and lists it.

T F **8.** An adequate system of internal control over cash will provide for safeguarding both incoming and outgoing funds.

T F **9.** Both checks and cash may be listed on the deposit slip.

T F **10.** Checks can be identified on a deposit slip by the use of the American Bankers Association transit numbers.

T F **11.** Each petty cash payment is entered separately in the general journal.

T F **12.** Checks made payable to cash or to bearer need not be endorsed when deposited.

T F **13.** The petty cash analysis sheet is a memorandum record of petty cash payments rather than a record of original entry.

T F **14.** Once created, login information for online bank account access should not be changed.

T F **15.** The check to replenish the petty cash fund is written for an amount sufficient to restore the fund to its established balance.

T F **16.** The money represented by deposited checks becomes available for use as soon as the deposit is made.

Part B Matching *For each numbered item, choose the matching term from the box and write the identifying letter in the answer column.*

a. NSF Check
b. Deposit in Transit
c. Outstanding checks
d. Bank reconciliation
e. Bank statement
f. Stub
g. Payee
h. Drawer
i. Deposit slip
j. Promissory note
k. Petty cash fund
l. Internal control
m. EFT

______ **1.** A check on which payment has been refused because of too few funds in the issuer's account.

______ **2.** Checks issued and recorded that have not been paid by the bank.

______ **3.** A written promise to pay a specific amount at a specific time.

______ **4.** A fund used for payments involving small amounts of money.

______ **5.** A system designed to safeguard assets and to help ensure the accuracy and reliability of accounting records.

______ **6.** Receipts that have been deposited and entered in the firm's accounting records but have not yet been entered on the bank's records.

______ **7.** A form received from the bank showing all transactions recorded in the depositor's account during the month.

______ **8.** The form that contains all the information necessary for journalizing a transaction paid by check.

______ **9.** The person or firm from whose account a check is to be paid.

______ **10.** The firm or person designated on the check to receive payment.

______ **11.** The process of determining why a difference exists between the firm's accounting records and the bank records and bringing them into balance.

______ **12.** A form on which all cash and cash items are listed before they are placed in the bank.

______ **13.** An electronic transfer of money from one account to another.

Demonstration Problem

On June 2, 2016, Rancho Santiago Legal Services received its May bank statement. Enclosed with the bank statement, shown below, was a debit memorandum for $150 for a NSF check issued by James Greene bill. Additionally, check 177 was correctly drawn for $400 in payment of a utility bill, but was mistakenly recorded by Rancho Sangtiago Legal Services as $40. The firm's checkbook contained the information shown below about deposits made and checks issued during May. The balance of the **Cash** account and the checkbook on May 31 was $37,345.

Instructions

1. Prepare a bank reconciliation statement for Rancho Santiago Legal Services as of May 31, 2016.
2. Record general journal entries for any items on the bank reconciliation statement that must be journalized. Date the entries May 31, 2016. Number the journal as page 17.

Checkbook information:

May 1	Balance	$40,592
1	Check 177	40
1	Check 178	800
7	Deposit	2,600
8	Check 179	900
12	Check 180	6,000
17	Check 181	720
19	Deposit	680
22	Check 182	88
23	Check 183	592
26	Deposit	1,848
29	Check 184	160
31	Deposit	925
		$37,345

First California National Bank

Rancho Santiago Legal Services
4312 Brea Street
Yorba Linda, CA 92885-8714

ACCOUNT NO. 77546798
PERIOD ENDING: May 31, 2016

CHECK NO.	AMOUNT	DATE	DESCRIPTION	BALANCE
			Balance last statement	40,592.00
177	400.00	6/1		40,192.00
178	800.00	6/4		39,392.00
	2,600.00	6/7	Deposit	41,992.00
179	900.00	6/8		41,092.00
180	6,000.00	6/12		35,092.00
	150.00	6/12	Debit Memorandum	34,942.00
181	720.00	6/17		34,222.00
	680.00	6/19	Deposit	34,902.00
182	88.00	6/22		34,814.00
	1,848.00	6/26	Deposit	36,662.00
	25.00	6/29	Service Charge	36,637.00

SOLUTION

Rancho Santiago Legal Services
Bank Reconciliation Statement
May 31, 2016

Balance on Bank Statement		36,637.00
Additions:		
Deposit of May 31 in Transit		925.00
		37,562.00
Deductions for Outstanding Checks:		
Check 183 of May 23	592.00	
Check 184 of May 29	160.00	
Total Checks Outstanding		752.00
Adjusted Bank Balance		36,810.00
Balance in Books		37,345.00
Deductions:		
NSF Check	150.00	
Recording error, Check 177	360.00	
Bank Service Charge	25.00	535.00
Adjusted Book Balance		36,810.00

GENERAL JOURNAL PAGE 17

	DATE		DESCRIPTION	POST. REF.	DEBIT	CREDIT	
1	2016						1
2	May	31	Accounts Receivable/James Greene		150.00		2
3			Cash			150.00	3
4			To record NSF check returned by bank				4
5							5
6		31	Miscellaneous Expense		25.00		6
7			Cash			25.00	7
8			To record bank service charge for May				8
9							9
10		31	Utilities Expense		360.00		10
11			Cash			360.00	11
12			To correct error for check 177 of May 1.				12
13							13
14							14

WORKING PAPERS

Name ______________________________

EXERCISES 9.1

GENERAL JOURNAL

PAGE ______

	DATE		DESCRIPTION	POST. REF.	DEBIT	CREDIT	
1							1
2							2
3							3
4							4
5							5
6							6
7							7
8							8
9							9
10							10

EXERCISES 9.2

GENERAL JOURNAL

PAGE ______

	DATE		DESCRIPTION	POST. REF.	DEBIT	CREDIT	
1							1
2							2
3							3
4							4
5							5

Name ______________________

EXERCISE 9.3

GENERAL JOURNAL

PAGE ______

	DATE		DESCRIPTION	POST. REF.	DEBIT	CREDIT	
1							1
2							2
3							3
4							4
5							5
6							6
7							7
8							8
9							9
10							10
11							11
12							12

EXERCISE 9.4

Name ______________________

GENERAL JOURNAL PAGE ______

	DATE		DESCRIPTION	POST. REF.	DEBIT	CREDIT	
1							1
2							2
3							3
4							4
5							5
6							6
7							7
8							8
9							9
10							10
11							11
12							12
13							13
14							14

EXERCISE 9.5

	Bank Balance	Book Balance	Accounting Entry
1.			
2.			
3.			
4.			
5.			
6.			
7.			

Name

EXERCISE 9.6

Name

EXERCISE 9.6 (continued)

GENERAL JOURNAL PAGE

	DATE		DESCRIPTION	POST. REF.	DEBIT	CREDIT	
1							1
2							2
3							3
4							4
5							5
6							6
7							7
8							8
9							9
10							10
11							11
12							12

EXERCISE 9.7

Name ______________________________

EXERCISE 9.8

GENERAL JOURNAL PAGE 21

	DATE	DESCRIPTION	POST. REF.	DEBIT	CREDIT	
1						1
2						2
3						3
4						4
5						5
6						6
7						7
8						8
9						9
10						10
11						11
12						12
13						13
14						14
15						15
16						16
17						17
18						18

Name

PROBLEM 9.1A

GENERAL JOURNAL

PAGE ______

DATE		DESCRIPTION	POST. REF.	DEBIT	CREDIT

Name ____________________

GENERAL LEDGER

ACCOUNT ____________________ ACCOUNT NO. ________

DATE		DESCRIPTION	POST. REF.	DEBIT	CREDIT	BALANCE DEBIT	BALANCE CREDIT

Analyze: ____________________

PROBLEM 9.2A

GENERAL JOURNAL PAGE ________

	DATE		DESCRIPTION	POST. REF.	DEBIT	CREDIT	
1							1
2							2
3							3
4							4
5							5
6							6
7							7
8							8
9							9
10							10
11							11
12							12

Name ______________________

PROBLEM 9.2A (continued)

PETTY CASH ANALYSIS SHEET

PAGE ____

DATE	VOU. NO.	DESCRIPTION	RECEIPTS	PAYMENTS	DISTRIBUTION OF PAYMENTS				
					SUPPLIES DEBIT	DELIVERY EXPENSE DEBIT	MISC. EXPENSE DEBIT	OTHER ACCOUNTS DEBIT	
								ACCOUNT NAME	AMOUNT

Analyze: ______________________

Name

PROBLEM 9.3A

GENERAL JOURNAL PAGE

	DATE		DESCRIPTION	POST. REF.	DEBIT	CREDIT	
1							1
2							2
3							3
4							4
5							5
6							6
7							7
8							8
9							9
10							10
11							11
12							12
13							13

Analyze:

Name

PROBLEM 9.4A

Name

PROBLEM 9.4A (continued)

GENERAL JOURNAL

PAGE

DATE		DESCRIPTION	POST. REF.	DEBIT	CREDIT

Analyze:

Name

PROBLEM 9.5A

GENERAL JOURNAL

PAGE

	DATE		DESCRIPTION	POST. REF.	DEBIT	CREDIT	
1							1
2							2
3							3
4							4
5							5
6							6
7							7
8							8
9							9
10							10
11							11
12							12
13							13

Analyze:

Name

PROBLEM 9.6A

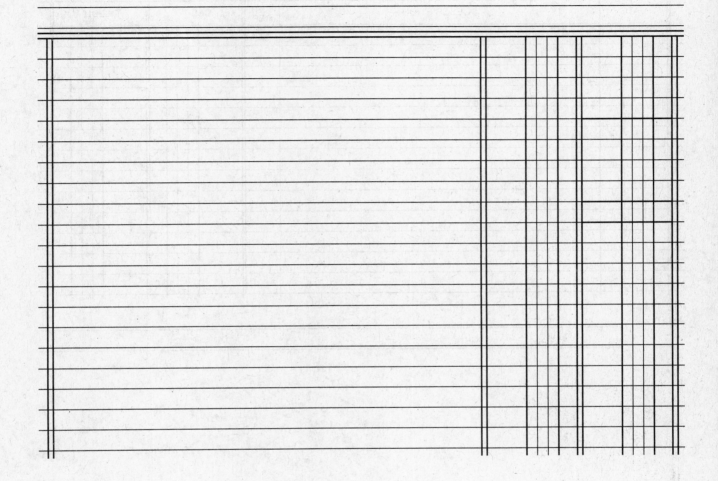

Name

PROBLEM 9.6A (continued)

GENERAL JOURNAL PAGE

	DATE		DESCRIPTION	POST. REF.	DEBIT	CREDIT	
1							1
2							2
3							3
4							4
5							5
6							6
7							7
8							8
9							9
10							10
11							11
12							12
13							13

Analyze:

Name ______________________

PROBLEM 9.1B

GENERAL JOURNAL

PAGE ______

DATE		DESCRIPTION	POST. REF.	DEBIT	CREDIT

Name ______________________

GENERAL LEDGER

ACCOUNT ______________________ ACCOUNT NO. ______

DATE		DESCRIPTION	POST. REF.	DEBIT	CREDIT	BALANCE	
						DEBIT	CREDIT

Analyze: ______________________

PROBLEM 9.2B

GENERAL JOURNAL PAGE ______

	DATE		DESCRIPTION	POST. REF.	DEBIT	CREDIT	
1							1
2							2
3							3
4							4
5							5
6							6
7							7
8							8
9							9
10							10
11							11
12							12

Name ____________________

PROBLEM 9.2B (continued)

PETTY CASH ANALYSIS SHEET

PAGE ____

DATE	VOU. NO.	DESCRIPTION	RECEIPTS	PAYMENTS	DISTRIBUTION OF PAYMENTS				
					SUPPLIES DEBIT	DELIVERY EXPENSE DEBIT	MISC. EXPENSE DEBIT	OTHER ACCOUNTS DEBIT	
								ACCOUNT NAME	AMOUNT

Analyze: ____________________

Name

PROBLEM 9.3B

GENERAL JOURNAL PAGE

	DATE		DESCRIPTION	POST. REF.	DEBIT	CREDIT	
1							1
2							2
3							3
4							4
5							5
6							6
7							7
8							8
9							9
10							10
11							11
12							12
13							13

Analyze:

Name

PROBLEM 9.4B

Name ____________________

PROBLEM 9.4B (continued)

GENERAL JOURNAL PAGE ______

DATE		DESCRIPTION	POST. REF.	DEBIT	CREDIT

Analyze: ____________________

Name

PROBLEM 9.5B

GENERAL JOURNAL PAGE

	DATE	DESCRIPTION	POST. REF.	DEBIT	CREDIT	
1						1
2						2
3						3
4						4
5						5
6						6
7						7
8						8
9						9
10						10
11						11
12						12
13						13

Analyze:

Name

PROBLEM 9.6B

Name ____________________

PROBLEM 9.6B (continued)

GENERAL JOURNAL PAGE ______

	DATE		DESCRIPTION	POST. REF.	DEBIT	CREDIT	
1							1
2							2
3							3
4							4
5							5
6							6
7							7
8							8
9							9
10							10
11							11
12							12
13							13

Analyze: ____________________

Name

CRITICAL THINKING PROBLEM 9.1

1.

DATE	CASH COUNT	LESS: CHANGE FUND	BANK DEPOSIT

DATE	BANK DEPOSIT	SALES, PER THE CASH REGISTER TAPE	AMOUNT SHORT

2.

GENERAL JOURNAL PAGE ____

	DATE		DESCRIPTION	POST. REF.	DEBIT	CREDIT	
1							1
2							2
3							3
4							4

3.

Name

CRITICAL THINKING PROBLEM 9.2

Name

CRITICAL THINKING PROBLEM 9.2 (continued)

Chapter 9 Practice Test Answer Key

Part A True-False

1.	T	12.	F
2.	F	13.	T
3.	F	14.	F
4.	F	15.	T
5.	T	16.	F
6.	F		
7.	F		
8.	T		
9.	T		
10.	T		
11.	F		

Part B Matching

1. a
2. c
3. j
4. k
5. l
6. b
7. e
8. f
9. h
10. g
11. d
12. i
13. m

CHAPTER 10

Payroll Computations, Records, and Payment

STUDY GUIDE

Understanding the Chapter

Objectives

1. Explain the major federal laws relating to employee earnings and withholding. **2.** Compute gross earnings of employees. **3.** Determine employee deductions for social security taxes. **4.** Determine employee deductions for Medicare taxes. **5.** Determine employee deductions for income taxes. **6.** Enter gross earnings, deductions, and net pay in the payroll register. **7.** Journalize payroll transactions in the general journal. **8.** Maintain an earnings record for each employee. **9.** Define the accounting terms new to this chapter.

Reading Assignment

Read Chapter 10 in the textbook. Complete the Section Self Review as you finish reading each section of the chapter, and the Comprehensive Self Review at the end of the chapter. Refer to the Chapter 10 Glossary or to the Glossary at the end of the book to find definitions for terms that are not familiar to you.

Activities

❑ **Thinking Critically** — Answer the *Thinking Critically* questions for H&R Block and Managerial Implications.

❑ **Discussion Questions** — Answer each assigned review question in Chapter 10.

❑ **Exercises** — Complete each assigned exercise in Chapter 10. Use the forms provided in this SGWP. The objectives covered by an exercise are given after the exercise number. If you need help with an exercise, review the portion of the chapter related to the objective(s) covered.

❑ **Problems A/B** — Complete each assigned problem in Chapter 10. Use the forms provided in this SGWP. The objectives covered by a problem are given after the problem number. If you need help with a problem, review the portion of the chapter related to the objective(s) covered.

❑ **Critical Thinking Problems** — Complete the critical thinking problems as assigned. Use the forms provided in this SGWP.

❑ **Business Connections** — Complete the Business Connections activities as assigned to gain a deeper understanding of Chapter 10 concepts.

Practice Tests

Complete the Practice Tests, which cover the main points in your reading assignment. Compare your answers with those in the Practice Test Answer Key for Chapter 10 at the end of this chapter. If you have answered any questions incorrectly, review the related section of the text.

Part A True-False *For each of the following statements, circle T in the answer column if the statement is true or F if the statement is false.*

T F **1.** The Fair Labor Standards Act fixes a minimum wage for supervisory employees paid a monthly salary.

T F **2.** Payroll taxes apply to salaries and wages paid to employees and to amounts paid independent contractors.

T F **3.** Employees can choose whether they want to be covered by the social security laws.

T F **4.** Most employers determine the amount of income tax to be withheld from the employee's pay by using withholding tables.

T F **5.** The state unemployment tax rate can be reduced by the rate charged by the federal government in the federal unemployment tax program.

T F **6.** The employee's marital status, number of exemptions, earnings for the pay period, and length of pay period are all factors in determining the amount of social security tax to be withheld.

T F **7.** The employer is required to contribute the same amount of federal unemployment tax as the amount withheld from the employee's earnings.

T F **8.** The Medicare tax is included in the social security tax (OASDI).

T F **9.** The workers' compensation program is a federal program.

T F **10.** The payroll register provides all the information required to make a general journal entry to record the payroll.

T F **11.** An employee worked 44 hours during the week. Her regular hourly pay is $10 per hour. Her gross pay for the week is $440.00.

T F **12.** A company hires Charles Alexander, CPA, to prepare monthly financial statements. Alexander comes to the company's office, reviews source documents, and later returns the statements. He would be classified as an employee.

Part B Matching *For each numbered item, choose the matching term from the box and write the identifying letter in the answer column.*

______	**1.** A record for each employee showing the person's earnings and deductions for the period, along with cumulative data.	**a.** Employee earnings record
______	**2.** Deductions to pay for medical benefits for retired persons.	**b.** Payroll register
______	**3.** A tax levied on the employer to provide benefits to employees who lose their jobs.	**c.** Exempt wages
______	**4.** A government publication containing withholding tables for employee taxes.	**d.** Workers' compensation insurance
______	**5.** Wages before deductions.	**e.** Overtime
______	**6.** Wages paid in a year above the base amount subject to a tax.	**f.** Circular E
______	**7.** A columnar record that shows each employee's earnings, deductions, and net pay.	**g.** Medicare premiums
______	**8.** Time worked in excess of 40 hours per week.	**h.** Unemployment tax
______	**9.** Provides for funding of retirement and disability benefits.	**i.** Federal Insurance Contributions Act
______	**10.** The form that employees file in order to claim the number of allowances to which they are entitled.	**j.** Employee's Withholding Allowance Certificate Form W4
		k. Gross pay

Demonstration Problem

HR4u Consulting Company pays its employees monthly. Payments made by the company on November 30, 2016, follow. Cumulative amounts paid to the persons named prior to November 30 are also given.

1. Alexia Arciero, President, gross monthly salary of $17,000; gross earnings prior to November 30, $170,000.
2. Virginia Richey, Vice President, gross monthly salary of $14,000; gross earnings paid prior to November 30, $140,000.
3. Michael Price, independent accountant who audits the company's accounts, $17,500; gross amounts paid prior to November 30, $5,000.
4. Evelyn Wu, Treasurer, gross monthly salary of $10,060; gross earnings prior to November 30, $100,000.
5. Payment to Hankins Research Services for monthly services of Robert Hankins, a tax consultant, $7,000; amount paid to Hankins Research Services prior to November 30, $24,000.

Instructions

1. Use an earnings ceiling of $113,700, and a tax rate of 6.2 percent for social security taxes and a tax rate of 1.45 percent on all earnings for medicare taxes. Prepare a schedule showing:
   a. Each employee's cumulative earnings prior to November 30.
   b. Each employee's gross earnings for November.
   c. The amounts to be withheld for each payroll tax from each employee's earnings; the employee's income tax withholdings are Arciero, $5,500; Richey, $3,250; Wu, $1,250.
   d. The net amount due each employee.
   e. The total gross earnings, the total of each payroll tax deduction, and the total net amount payable to employees.
2. Give the general journal entry to record the company's payroll on November 30. Use journal page 34. Omit description.
3. Give the general journal entry to record payments to employees on November 30.

SOLUTION

EARNINGS SCHEDULE

EMPLOYEE NAME	CUMULATIVE EARNINGS	MONTHLY PAY	SOCIAL SECURITY	MEDICARE	EMPLOYEE INCOME TAX WITHHOLDING	NET PAY
John Arciero	**$170,000.00**	**$17,000.00**	**—**	**$246.50**	**$5,500.00**	**$11,253.50**
Virginia Richey	**140,000.00**	**14,000.00**	**—**	**203.00**	**3,250.00**	**10,547.00**
Evelyn Wu	**100,000.00**	**10,000.00**	**620.00**	**145.00**	**1,250.00**	**7,985.00**
Totals	**$410,000.00**	**$41,000.00**	**$620.00**	**$594.50**	**$10,000.00**	**$29,785.50**

Michael Price and Robert Hankins are not employees of HR4u Consulting Company.

GENERAL JOURNAL PAGE **34**

DATE		DESCRIPTION	POST. REF.	DEBIT	CREDIT
2016					
Nov.	**30**	**Salaries Expense**		**41 0 0 0 00**	
		Social Security Tax Payable			**6 2 0 00**
		Medicare Tax Payable			**5 9 4 50**
		Employee Income Tax Payable			**1 0 0 0 0 00**
		Salaries Payable			**29 7 8 5 50**
	30	**Salaries Payable**		**29 7 8 5 50**	
		Cash			**29 7 8 5 50**

WORKING PAPERS

Name ____________________

EXERCISE 10.1

EMPLOYEE NO.	HOURLY RATE	HOURS WORKED	GROSS EARNINGS

EXERCISE 10.2

HOURLY RATE	OVERTIME RATE	REGULAR HOURS WORKED	OVERTIME HOURS WORKED	REGULAR PAY	OVERTIME PAY	GROSS PAY

EXERCISE 10.3

EMPLOYEE NO.	DECEMBER SALARY	YEAR TO DATE EARNINGS THROUGH NOVEMBER 30	SOC. SEC. TAXABLE EARNINGS-DECEMBER	SOCIAL SECURITY TAX 6.20%

EXERCISE 10.4

EMPLOYEE NO.	DECEMBER SALARY	MEDICARE TAXABLE EARNINGS-DECEMBER	MEDICARE TAX 1.45%

EXERCISE 10.5

EMPLOYEE NO.	MARITAL STATUS	WITHHOLDING ALLOWANCES	WEEKLY SALARY	INCOME TAX WITHHOLDING

Name ____________________

EXERCISE 10.6

GENERAL JOURNAL

PAGE ______

	DATE		DESCRIPTION	POST. REF.	DEBIT	CREDIT	
1							1
2							2
3							3
4							4
5							5
6							6
7							7
8							8
9							9
10							10
11							11
12							12
13							13
14							14
15							15

EXERCISE 10.7

GENERAL JOURNAL

PAGE ______

	DATE		DESCRIPTION	POST. REF.	DEBIT	CREDIT	
1							1
2							2
3							3
4							4
5							5
6							6
7							7
8							8
9							9
10							10
11							11
12							12
13							13
14							14
15							15

Name ____________________

PROBLEM 10.1A or 10.1B

EMPLOYEE NO.	REGULAR HOURS, HOURLY RATE	HOURS WORKED	REGULAR TIME EARNINGS	OVERTIME EARNINGS	GROSS EARNINGS

Gross Pay	
Social Security Tax	
Medicare Tax	
Income Tax Withholding	
Health & Disability	
Charitable Contribution	
Savings	
Net Pay	

GENERAL JOURNAL

PAGE ____

	DATE		DESCRIPTION	POST. REF.	DEBIT	CREDIT	
1							1
2							2
3							3
4							4
5							5

Analyze: ____________________

Name ______________________________

PROBLEM 10.2A or 10.2B

PAYROLL REGISTER WEEK BEGINNING ________ AND ENDING ________ PAID ________

NAME	NO. OF ALLOW.	MARITAL STATUS	CUMULATIVE EARNINGS	NO. OF HRS.	RATE	EARNINGS			CUMULATIVE EARNINGS	TAXABLE WAGES			DEDUCTIONS			NET AMOUNT	DISTRIBUTION	
						REGULAR TIME EARNINGS	OVERTIME EARNINGS	GROSS AMOUNT		SOCIAL SECURITY	MEDICARE	FUTA	SOCIAL SECURITY	MEDICARE	INCOME TAX		CHECK NO.	WAGES EXPENSE

Name

PROBLEM 10.2A or 10.2B (continued)

GENERAL JOURNAL PAGE

DATE		DESCRIPTION	POST. REF.	DEBIT	CREDIT

Analyze:

Name ______________________

PROBLEM 10.3A or 10.3B

PAYROLL REGISTER WEEK BEGINNING ______ AND ENDING ______ PAID ______

NAME	NO. OF ALLOW.	MARITAL STATUS	CUMULATIVE EARNINGS	NO. OF HRS.	RATE	EARNINGS			CUMULATIVE EARNINGS
						REGULAR TIME EARNINGS	OVERTIME EARNINGS	GROSS AMOUNT	

TAXABLE WAGES		FUTA	DEDUCTIONS			NET AMOUNT	CHECK NO.	DISTRIBUTION	
SOCIAL SECURITY	MEDICARE		SOCIAL SECURITY	MEDICARE	INCOME TAX			OFFICE WAGES	DELIVERY WAGES

Name ____________________

PROBLEM 10.3A or 10.3B (continued)

GENERAL JOURNAL PAGE ______

	DATE		DESCRIPTION	POST. REF.	DEBIT	CREDIT	
1							1
2							2
3							3
4							4
5							5
6							6
7							7
8							8
9							9
10							10
11							11
12							12
13							13
14							14
15							15
16							16
17							17
18							18
19							19
20							20
21							21
22							22
23							23
24							24
25							25
26							26
27							27
28							28
29							29
30							30
31							31
32							32
33							33
34							34

Analyze: ____________________

____

Name ____________________

PROBLEM 10.4A or 10.4B

EMPLOYEE NAME	CUMULATIVE EARNINGS	MONTHLY PAY	SOCIAL SECURITY	MEDICARE	EMPLOYEE INCOME TAX WITHHOLDING	NET PAY
Totals						

GENERAL JOURNAL

PAGE ______

DATE	DESCRIPTION	POST. REF.	DEBIT	CREDIT

Analyze: ____________________

Name ______________________

CRITICAL THINKING PROBLEM 10.1

EMPLOYEE NAME	CUMULATIVE EARNINGS	MONTHLY PAY	SOCIAL SECURITY	MEDICARE	EMPLOYEE INCOME TAX WITHHOLDING	NET PAY

GENERAL JOURNAL PAGE ______

	DATE		DESCRIPTION	POST. REF.	DEBIT	CREDIT	
1							1
2							2
3							3
4							4
5							5
6							6
7							7
8							8
9							9
10							10
11							11
12							12
13							13
14							14
15							15

Analyze: ______________________

Name

CRITICAL THINKING PROBLEM 10.2

Chapter 10 Practice Test Answer Key

Part A True-False

1. F
2. F
3. F
4. T
5. F
6. F
7. F
8. F
9. F
10. T
11. F
12. F

Part B Matching

1. a
2. g
3. h
4. f
5. k
6. c
7. b
8. e
9. i
10. j

CHAPTER 11

Payroll Taxes, Deposits, and Reports

STUDY GUIDE

Understanding the Chapter

Objectives

1. Explain how and when payroll taxes are paid to the government. **2.** Compute and record the employer's social security and Medicare taxes. **3.** Record deposit of social security, Medicare, and employee income taxes. **4.** Prepare an Employer's Quarterly Federal Tax Return, Form 941. **5.** Prepare Wage and Tax Statement (Form W-2) and Annual Transmittal of Wage and Tax Statements (Form W-3). **6.** Compute and record liability for federal and state unemployment taxes and record payment of the taxes. **7.** Prepare an Employer's Federal Unemployment Tax Return, Form 940 or 940-EZ. **8.** Compute and record workers' compensation insurance premiums. **9.** Define the accounting terms new to this chapter.

Reading Assignment

Read Chapter 11 in the textbook. Complete the textbook Section Self Review as you finish reading each section of the chapter, and Comprehensive Self Review at the end of the chapter. Refer to the Chapter 11 Glossary or to the Glossary at the end of the book to find definitions for terms that are not familiar to you.

Activities

- ❑ **Thinking Critically** — Answer the *Thinking Critically* questions for Marek Brothers Systems, Inc. and Resorts and Managerial Implications.
- ❑ **Discussion Questions** — Answer each assigned discussion question in Chapter 11.
- ❑ **Exercises** — Complete each assigned exercise in Chapter 11. Use the forms provided in this SGWP. The objectives covered by an exercise are given after the exercise number. If you need help with an exercise, review the portion of the chapter related to the objective(s) covered.
- ❑ **Problems A/B** — Complete each assigned problem in Chapter 11. Use the forms provided in this SGWP. The objectives covered by a problem are given after the problem number. If you need help with a problem, review the portion of the chapter related to the objective(s) covered.
- ❑ **Critical Thinking Problems** — Complete the critical thinking problems as assigned. Use the forms provided in this SGWP.
- ❑ **Business Connections** — Complete the Business Connections activities as assigned to gain a deeper understanding of Chapter 11 concepts.

Practice Tests

Complete the Practice Tests, which cover the main points in your reading assignment. Compare your answers with those in the Practice Test Answer Key for Chapter 11 at the end of this chapter. If you have answered any questions incorrectly, review the related section of the text.

Part A True-False *For each of the following statements, circle T in the answer column if the statement is true or F if the statement is false.*

T F **1.** Employers with a small number of employees are frequently required to deposit the entire amount of estimated workers' compensation insurance premiums early in the year.

T F **2.** The credit against the federal unemployment tax is the amount actually paid to the state under its unemployment compensation insurance program.

T F **3.** The premium on workers' compensation insurance is based on the federal unemployment tax.

T F **4.** Premiums on workers' compensation insurance vary with the type of work performed by employees.

T F **5.** The federal unemployment tax for the year is based on an audit of the payroll for the year.

T F **6.** Under a typical state plan, the federal government actually receives 0.8 percent of the taxable wages because the employer is allowed credits for payments made to the state.

T F **7.** The federal government grants a lower federal unemployment rate under an experience rating system to those employers who provide stable employment.

T F **8.** Most states allow a credit against the FUTA for amounts paid to the federal government as SUTA.

T F **9.** The employer's payroll taxes are usually recorded at the end of each payroll period, even though the cash will not be paid out until later.

T F **10.** A business firm pays income tax withholding at the same rate and on the same taxable wages as employees.

T F **11.** During the month immediately following the close of each calendar quarter, an employer is required to file a quarterly tax report and pay in or deposit any balance owed for social security and Medicare taxes and employees' income tax withheld.

T F **12.** On each date of payment of an employee's wages, the employer must provide the employee with a statement, on Form W-2, of earnings and taxes withheld.

T F **13.** Employees' individual earnings records provide much of the information needed to prepare the Employer's Quarterly Federal Tax Return, Form 941.

T F **14.** Only the amount of each employee's earnings up to $7,000 each year is subject to the social security tax.

T F **15.** Payments of social security tax, Medicare tax, and employee income tax withheld may be deposited, without penalty, in an authorized depository at any time up to January 31 of the following year.

T F **16.** The employee must attach a Form W-3 to his or her federal income tax return.

T F **17.** Each employer subject to the Federal Unemployment Compensation Tax Act must file an annual return on Form 940 by January 15 of the following year.

T F **18.** Social security taxes are paid by the employer but not the employee.

Part B Matching *For each number item, choose the matching term from the box and write the identifying letter in the answer column.*

a. Workers' compensation
b. Form 8109
c. Form 941
d. Form 940
e. Form W-3
f. Form W-2
g. Experience rating system
h. Publication 15, Circular E
i. Federal unemployment tax
j. Medicare tax

_____ **1.** A tax borne equally by the employer and employee.

_____ **2.** A tax paid solely by the employer.

_____ **3.** An IRS publication containing tax rates and other information about payroll taxes.

_____ **4.** Plan providing benefits to employees who are injured or become ill on the job.

_____ **5.** A plan under which the SUTA is adjusted to reflect the unemployment experience of the employer.

_____ **6.** A yearly form sent to the U.S. government summarizing earnings and payroll taxes withheld for the year.

_____ **7.** A statement of earnings and deductions for each employee.

_____ **8.** A deposit "coupon" accompanying the employer's deposit of taxes in a commercial bank.

_____ **9.** An annual report to the federal government summarizing the employer's unemployment compensation tax for the year.

_____ **10.** A quarterly report to the federal government summarizing taxable wages and payroll taxes due for the quarter.

Demonstration Problem

The payroll register of the USA Printing and Copy Center showed employee earnings of $16,000 for the month ended January 31, 2016. Employee income tax withholding was $2,400. Use a social security rate of 6.2%, Medicare rate of 1.45%, FUTA rate of 0.6%, and SUTA rate of 5.4%. Assure all earnings are subject to these taxes.

Instructions

1. Compute the employees' social security and Medicare taxes.
2. Record the payroll for January in the general journal, page 3.
3. Compute the employer's payroll taxes for the period.
4. Prepare a general journal entry to record the employer's payroll taxes for the period.
5. Prepare a general journal entry to record the February 4 deposit of the social security, Medicare, and employee income taxes for the month.

SOLUTION

CALCULATION OF EMPLOYEE TAXES

Social security: 0.062 × $16,000	**$992.00**
Medicare: 0.0145 × $16,000	**232.00**
	$1,224.00

CALCULATION OF EMPLOYER TAXES

Social security: 0.062 × $16,000	**$992.00**
Medicare: 0.0145 × $16,000	**232.00**
FUTA: 0.006 × $16,000	**96.00**
SUTA: 0.054 × $16,000	**864.00**
	$2,184.00

SOLUTION (continued)

GENERAL JOURNAL PAGE 3

DATE		DESCRIPTION	POST. REF.	DEBIT	CREDIT
2016					
Jan.	31	**Salaries Expense**		16000 00	
		Social Security Tax Payable			992 00
		Medicare Tax Payable			232 00
		Employee Income Tax Payable			2400 00
		Salaries Payable			12376 00
		Payroll for January			
	31	**Payroll Tax Expense**		2184 00	
		Social Security Tax Payable			992 00
		Medicare Tax Payable			232 00
		Federal Unemployment Tax Payable			96 00
		State Unemployment Tax Payable			864 00
		Payroll for January			
Feb.	4	**Social Security Tax Payable**		1984 00	
		Medicare Tax Payable		464 00	
		Employee Income Tax Payable		2400 00	
		Cash			4848 00
		Deposit of payroll taxes withholding			

WORKING PAPERS

Name ____________________

EXERCISE 11.1

EXERCISE 11.2

GENERAL JOURNAL

PAGE ______

	DATE		DESCRIPTION	POST. REF.	DEBIT	CREDIT	
1							1
2							2
3							3
4							4
5							5
6							6
7							7

EXERCISE 11.3

TAX	BASE	RATE	AMOUNT

EXERCISE 11.4

GENERAL JOURNAL

PAGE ______

	DATE		DESCRIPTION	POST. REF.	DEBIT	CREDIT	
1							1
2							2
3							3
4							4
5							5
6							6
7							7

Name ______________________

EXERCISE 11.5

____

____

____

EXERCISE 11.6

GENERAL JOURNAL — PAGE ______

	DATE	DESCRIPTION	POST. REF.	DEBIT	CREDIT	
1						1
2						2
3						3
4						4
5						5
6						6
7						7

EXERCISE 11.7

____

____

____

____

EXERCISE 11.8

WORK CLASSIFICATION	ESTIMATED EARNINGS	RATE	ESTIMATED PREMIUM

Name ____________________

PROBLEM 11.1A or 11.1B

TAX	BASE	RATE	AMOUNT

GENERAL JOURNAL PAGE 28

	DATE		DESCRIPTION	POST. REF.	DEBIT	CREDIT	
1							1
2							2
3							3
4							4
5							5
6							6
7							7
8							8
9							9
10							10
11							11
12							12

Analyze: ____________________

Name

PROBLEM 11.2A or 11.2B

GENERAL JOURNAL

PAGE

DATE	DESCRIPTION	POST. REF.	DEBIT	CREDIT

Analyze:

Name

PROBLEM 11.3A or 11.3B

GENERAL JOURNAL

PAGE

DATE		DESCRIPTION	POST. REF.	DEBIT	CREDIT

Analyze:

Name ______________________

PROBLEM 11.3A or 11.3B (continued)

Form **941 for 2016: Employer's Quarterly Federal Tax Return** 9901

Department of the Treasury — Internal Revenue Service

OMB No. 1545-0029

Employer identification number [ ][ ] — [ ][ ][ ][ ][ ][ ][ ]

Name *(not your trade name)* ______________________

Trade name *(if any)* ______________________

Address ______________________

Number Street Suite or room number

City State ZIP code

Report for this Quarter ...
(Check one.)

☐ **1:** January, February, March

☒ **2:** April, May, June

☐ **3:** July, August, September

☐ **4:** October, November, December

Read the separate instructions before you fill out this form. Please type or print within the boxes.

Part 1: Answer these questions for this quarter.

1 **Number of employees who received wages, tips, or other compensation for the pay period including:** ***Mar. 16*** **(Quarter 1),** ***June 16*** **(Quarter 2),** ***Sept. 16*** **(Quarter 3),** ***Dec. 16*** **(Quarter 4)** . . . 1 ______

2 **Wages, tips, and other compensation** . . . . 2 ______.

3 **Total income tax withheld from wages, tips, and other compensation** . . . . 3 ______.

4 **If no wages, tips, and other compensation are subject to social security or Medicare tax** . ☐ Check and go to line 6.

5 **Taxable social security and Medicare wages and tips:**

	Column 1		*Column 2*
5a **Taxable social security wages**	.	× .124 =	.
5b **Taxable social security tips**	.	× .124 =	.
5c **Taxable Medicare wages & tips**	.	× .029 =	.

5d **Total social security and Medicare taxes** (*Column 2,* lines 5a + 5b + 5c = line 5d) . 5d ______.

6 **Total taxes before adjustments** (lines 3 + 5d = line 6) . . . . 6 ______.

7 **Tax adjustments** (If your answer is a negative number, write it in brackets.):

7a **Current quarter's fractions of cents** . . . . ______.

7b **Current quarter's sick pay** . . . . ______.

7c **Current quarter's adjustments for tips and group-term life insurance** ______.

7d **Current year's income tax withholding** (Attach Form 941c) . . ______.

7e **Prior quarters' social security and Medicare taxes** (Attach Form 941c) ______.

7f **Special additions to federal income tax** (reserved use) . . . . ______.

7g **Special additions to social security and Medicare** (reserved use) ______.

7h **Total adjustments** (Combine all amounts: lines 7a through 7g.) . . . . 7h ______.

8 **Total taxes after adjustments** (Combine lines 6 and 7h.) . . . . 8 ______.

9 **Advance earned income credit (EIC) payments made to employees** . . . . 9 ______.

10 **Total taxes after adjustment for advance EIC** (lines 8 – 9 = line 10) . . . . 10 ______.

11 **Total deposits for this quarter, including overpayment applied from a prior quarter** . . 11 ______.

12 **Balance due** (lines 10 – 11 = line 12) Make checks payable to the *United States Treasury* . 12 ______.

13 **Overpayment** (If line 11 is more than line 10, write the difference here.) ______. Check one ☐ Apply to next return. ☐ Send a refund.

Next ➡

For Privacy Act and Paperwork Reduction Act Notice, see the back of the Payment Voucher. Cat. No. 17001Z Form **941**

Name

PROBLEM 11.3A or 11.3B (continued)

9902

Name *(not your trade name)* | Employer identification number

Part 2: Tell us about your deposit schedule for this quarter.

If you are unsure about whether you are a monthly schedule depositor or a semiweekly schedule depositor, see *Pub. 15 (Circular E)*, section 11.

14 ☐☐ **Write the state abbreviation for the state where you made your deposits** OR **write "MU" if you made your deposits in *multiple* states.**

15 **Check one:** ☐ **Line 10 is less than $2,500.** Go to Part 3.

☐ **You were a monthly schedule depositor for the entire quarter. Fill out your tax liability for each month.** Then go to Part 3.

Tax liability:		
	Month 1	.
	Month 2	.
	Month 3	.
	Total	. **Total must equal line 10.**

☐ **You were a semiweekly schedule depositor for any part of this quarter.** Fill out *Schedule B (Form 941): Report of Tax Liability for Semiweekly Schedule Depositors,* and attach it to this form.

Part 3: Tell us about your business. If a question does NOT apply to your business, leave it blank.

16 **If your business has closed and you do not have to file returns in the future** . . . . ☐ Check here, and

enter the final date you paid wages   /   / .

17 **If you are a seasonal employer and you do not have to file a return for every quarter of the year** . ☐ Check here.

Part 4: May we contact your third-party designee?

Do you want to allow an employee, a paid tax preparer, or another person to discuss this return with the IRS? See the instructions for details.

☐ Yes. Designee's name

Phone (   )   –   Personal Identification Number (PIN) ☐☐☐☐☐

☐ No.

Part 5: Sign here

Under penalties of perjury, I declare that I have examined this return, including accompanying schedules and statements, and to the best of my knowledge and belief, it is true, correct, and complete.

✗ Sign your name here

Print name and title

Date   /   /   Phone (   )   –

Part 6: For paid preparers only *(optional)*

Preparer's signature

Firm's name

Address   EIN

ZIP code

Date   /   /   Phone (   )   –   SSN/PTIN

☐ Check if you are self-employed.

Page **2**   Form **941**

Name

PROBLEM 11.4A or 11.4B

GENERAL JOURNAL

PAGE

DATE		DESCRIPTION	POST. REF.	DEBIT	CREDIT

Analyze:

Name ____________________

PROBLEM 11.5A or 11.5B

GENERAL JOURNAL

PAGE ______

DATE		DESCRIPTION	POST. REF.	DEBIT	CREDIT

Analyze: ____________________

Name

PROBLEM 11.5A or 11.5B (continued)

Form **940-EZ**

Department of the Treasury
Internal Revenue Service

Employer's Annual Federal Unemployment (FUTA) Tax Return

► See the separate Instructions for Form 940-EZ for information on completing this form.

OMB No. 1545-1110

2016

T	
FF	
FD	
FP	
I	
T	

You must complete this section. ►

Name (as distinguished from trade name) | Calendar year

Trade name, if any | Employer identification number (EIN)

Address (number and street) | City, state, and ZIP code

*Answer the questions under **Who May Use Form 940-EZ** on page 2. If you cannot use Form 940-EZ, you must use Form 940.*

A Enter the amount of contributions paid to your state unemployment fund (see the separate instructions) . . ► $ ____________

B (1) Enter the name of the state where you have to pay contributions . . . . ► ____________

(2) Enter your state reporting number as shown on your state unemployment tax return ►

If you will not have to file returns in the future, check here (see **Who Must File** in separate instructions) **and complete and sign the return.** ► ☐

If this is an Amended Return, check here (see **Amended Returns** in the separate instructions) . . . . ► ☐

Part I **Taxable Wages and FUTA Tax**

1	Total payments (including payments shown on lines 2 and 3) during the calendar year for services of employees			1	
2	Exempt payments. (Explain all exempt payments, attaching additional sheets if necessary.) ► ______________	2			
3	Payments of more than $7,000 for services. Enter only amounts over the first $7,000 paid to each employee **(see the separate instructions)**	3			
4	Add lines 2 and 3			4	
5	**Total taxable wages** (subtract line 4 from line 1) . . . . ►			5	
6	**FUTA tax.** Multiply the wages on line 5 by .006 and enter here. **(If the result is over $100, also complete Part II.)**			6	
7	Total FUTA tax deposited for the year, including any overpayment applied from a prior year			7	
8	**Balance due** (subtract line 7 from line 6). Pay to the "United States Treasury." . . . . ► If you owe more than $100, see **Depositing FUTA tax** in the separate instructions.			8	
9	**Overpayment** (subtract line 6 from line 7). Check if it is to be: ☐ **Applied to next return** or ☐ **Refunded** ►			9	

Part II **Record of Quarterly Federal Unemployment Tax Liability** (Do not include state liability.) **Complete only if line 6 is over $100.**

Quarter	First (Jan. 1 – Mar. 31)	Second (Apr. 1 – June 30)	Third (July 1 – Sept. 30)	Fourth (Oct. 1 – Dec. 31)	Total for year
Liability for quarter					

Third–Party Designee

Do you want to allow another person to discuss this return with the IRS (see the separate instructions)? ☐ **Yes.** Complete the following. ☐ **No**

Designee's name ► | Phone no. ► ( ) | Personal identification number (PIN) ►

Under penalties of perjury, I declare that I have examined this return, including accompanying schedules and statements, and, to the best of my knowledge and belief, it is true, correct, and complete, and that no part of any payment made to a state unemployment fund claimed as a credit was, or is to be, deducted from the payments to employees.

Signature ► | **Title (Owner, etc.)** ► | **Date** ►

For Privacy Act and Paperwork Reduction Act Notice, see the separate instructions. ▼ **DETACH HERE** ▼ Cat. No. 10983G Form **940-EZ**

Form **940-V(EZ)**

Department of the Treasury
Internal Revenue Service

Payment Voucher

Use this voucher only when making a payment with your return.

OMB No. 1545-1110

2016

Complete boxes 1, 2, and 3. Do not send cash, and do not staple your payment to this voucher. Make your check or money order payable to the "United States Treasury." Be sure to enter your employer identification number (EIN), "Form 940-EZ," and "2004" on your payment.

1 Enter your employer identification number (EIN).

2 **Enter the amount of your payment.** ► | Dollars | Cents

3 Enter your business name (individual name for sole proprietors).

Enter your address.

Enter your city, state, and ZIP code.

Name

PROBLEM 11.6A or 11.6B

WORK CLASSIFICATION	ESTIMATED EARNINGS	INSURANCE RATE	ESTIMATED PREMIUMS

WORK CLASSIFICATION	ACTUAL EARNINGS	INSURANCE RATE	ACTUAL PREMIUMS

Name

PROBLEM 11.6A or 11.6B (continued)

GENERAL JOURNAL PAGE

	DATE		DESCRIPTION	POST. REF.	DEBIT	CREDIT	
1							1
2							2
3							3
4							4
5							5
6							6
7							7
8							8
9							9
10							10
11							11
12							12
13							13
14							14
15							15
16							16
17							17
18							18
19							19

Analyze:

Name

CRITICAL THINKING PROBLEM 11.1

1.

2. YEARLY COST—CURRENT SYSTEM

CRITICAL THINKING PROBLEM 11.2

1.

2.

3.

4.

5.

Analyze:

Name

CRITICAL THINKING PROBLEM 11.2 (continued)

YEARLY COST—PROPOSED SYSTEM

3.

Chapter 11 Practice Test Answer Key

Part A True-False		Part B Matching
1. T	10. F	1. j
2. F	11. T	2. i
3. F	12. F	3. h
4. T	13. T	4. a
5. F	14. F	5. g
6. T	15. F	6. e
7. F	16. F	7. f
8. F	17. F	8. b
9. T	18. F	9. d
		10. c

CHAPTER 12

Accruals, Deferrals, and the Worksheet

STUDY GUIDE

Understanding the Chapter

Objectives

1. Determine the adjustment for merchandise inventory and enter the adjustment on the worksheet. **2.** Compute adjustments for accrued and prepaid expense items and enter the adjustments on the worksheet. **3.** Compute adjustments for accrued and deferred income items and enter the adjustments on the worksheet. **4.** Complete a ten-column worksheet. **5.** Define the accounting terms new to this chapter.

Reading Assignment

Read Chapter 12 in the textbook. Complete the textbook Section Self Review as you finish reading each section of the chapter, and the Comprehensive Self Review at the end of the chapter. Refer to the Chapter 12 Glossary or to the Glossary at the end of the book to find definitions for terms that are not familiar to you.

Activities

❑ **Thinking Critically** — Answer the *Thinking Critically* questions for Urban Outfitters and Managerial Implications.

❑ **Discussion Questions** — Answer each assigned discussion question in Chapter 12.

❑ **Exercises** — Complete each assigned exercise in Chapter 12. Use the forms provided in this SGWP. The objectives covered by an exercise are given after the exercise number. If you need help with an exercise, review the portion of the chapter related to the objective(s) covered.

❑ **Problems A/B** — Complete each assigned problem in Chapter 12. Use the forms provided in this SGWP. The objectives covered by a problem are given after the problem number. If you need help with a problem, review the portion of the chapter related to the objective(s) covered.

❑ **Critical Thinking Problems** — Complete the critical thinking problems as assigned. Use the forms provided in this SGWP.

❑ **Business Connections** — Complete the Business Connections activities as assigned to gain a deeper understanding of Chapter 12 concepts.

Practice Tests

Complete the Practice Tests, which cover the main points in your reading assignment. Compare your answers with those in the Practice Test Answer Key for Chapter 12 at the end of this chapter. If you have answered any questions incorrectly, review the related section of the text.

Part A True-False *For each of the following statements, circle T in the answer column if the statement is true or F if the statement is false.*

T F 1. The Adjusted Trial Balance column of the worksheet tests only the arithmetic accuracy of the worksheet to that point in the worksheet and statement preparation process.

T F 2. After the amounts shown in the Adjusted Trial Balance section have been extended, the difference between the total debits and total credits in the balance sheet section represents the net income or loss for the period.

T F 3. The accountant completes the worksheet and prepares the financial statements as soon as all adjustments have been entered on the worksheet.

T F 4. The net income for the business is entered as a debit entry in the Balance Sheet section and as a credit entry in the Income Statement section of the worksheet.

T F 5. Office or store supplies that have been paid for in cash do not need any adjusting entries.

T F 6. On the trial balance, the **Store Supplies** account shows a debit balance of $300. A physical count showed supplies on hand of $80. The adjusting entry includes a debit of $80 to the **Store Supplies Expense** account.

T F 7. An adjustment for depreciation results in an entry debiting the **Depreciation Expense** account and crediting the **Equipment** account.

T F 8. At the end of an accounting period, an adjustment is needed to record as an expense any part of the balance in an asset account that has been used up or has expired.

T F 9. The unadjusted trial balance figures for accumulated depreciation accounts do not include depreciation for the current period.

T F 10. The **Unearned Subscriptions Income** account will appear in the Liabilities section of the balance sheet.

T F 11. In the "adjustments" column of the worksheet, the **Merchandise Inventory** is debited for the amount of ending inventory and credited for the amount of beginning inventory.

T F 12. Under the accrual basis of accounting, purchases are recorded after the purchase has been paid.

T F 13. The **Interest Expense** account must be adjusted if an interest-bearing note payable is outstanding at the end of the fiscal period and interest has not been paid on that date.

T F 14. In most cases, **Prepaid Interest** will be classified in the Assets section on the balance sheet.

T F 15. The entry to record accrued interest on notes payable is a debit to **Interest Expense** and a credit to **Interest Receivable.**

T F 16. **Interest Receivable** is usually classified as a revenue account.

T F 17. Deferred income has been earned but not recorded, while accrued income has been recorded but not earned.

T F 18. Adjusting entries are recorded in the general journal after the worksheet and the financial statements are completed.

T F 19. The beginning merchandise inventory does not appear in the Adjusted Trial Balance.

T F 20. The **Drawing** account balance is extended to the Debit column in the Income Statement section.

T F 21. The financial statements are prepared directly from the worksheet.

T F 22. The statement of owner's equity should be prepared after the income statement is prepared.

T F 23. In preparing financial statements, it is unnecessary to make adjustments for relatively small items because they are immaterial and will not affect the statements.

T F 24. The accounts should be adjusted when preparing monthly or quarterly statements.

T F 25. A prepaid expense incorrectly charged to expense in an accounting period results in an understatement of net income in that period and an overstatement of net income in the following period.

Part B Exercise *In each of the following independent cases give the general journal entry to adjust the accounts for the year on December 31, 2016. Omit the descriptions.*

1. Store supplies costing $1,600 were purchased during the year and were charged to the **Store Supplies** account. At the end of the year, supplies costing $200 were on hand.

GENERAL JOURNAL PAGE______

	DATE		DESCRIPTION	POST. REF.	DEBIT	CREDIT	
1							1
2							2

2. On December 1, 2016 the company gave a $5,000 note payable to a supplier. The note bears interest at 6 percent.

GENERAL JOURNAL PAGE______

	DATE		DESCRIPTION	POST. REF.	DEBIT	CREDIT	
1							1
2							2

3. On October 1, 2016, the company received a four-month, 8 percent note for $3,500 from settlement of an overdue account. No interest has been recorded on the note.

GENERAL JOURNAL PAGE______

	DATE		DESCRIPTION	POST. REF.	DEBIT	CREDIT	
1							1
2							2

4. On November 1, 2016, the company purchased a one-year insurance policy for $8,400. The amount was charged to **Prepaid Insurance.**

GENERAL JOURNAL PAGE______

	DATE		DESCRIPTION	POST. REF.	DEBIT	CREDIT	
1							1
2							2

5. During 2016, the Irvine Quakes minor league hockey team received $1,200,000 from the sale of season tickets for 20 home games. The Unearned Season Tickets Income account was credited upon receipt of the cash. As of December 31, 8 home games had been played.

GENERAL JOURNAL PAGE______

	DATE		DESCRIPTION	POST. REF.	DEBIT	CREDIT	
1							1
2							2

Demonstration Problem

The trial balance for Pietro's Imports on December 31, 2016, the end of its accounting period, is shown on the worksheet.

Instructions

1. Complete the worksheet for the year, using the following information:
   - **a-b.** Ending merchandise inventory, $109,250.
   - **c.** Uncollectible accounts expense, $2,900.
   - **d.** Supplies on hand December 31, $2,780.
   - **e.** Depreciation on store equipment, $8,100.
   - **f.** Depreciation on office equipment, $5,875.
   - **g.** Accrued sales salaries, $4,000; accrued office salaries, $750.
   - **h.** Tax on accrued salaries: social security, $294.50; Medicare, $68.88.
2. Journalize the adjusting entries on page 16 of the general journal.

SOLUTION

Pietro's Imports
Worksheet
Year Ended December 31, 2016

ACCOUNT NAME	TRIAL BALANCE DEBIT	TRIAL BALANCE CREDIT	ADJUSTMENTS DEBIT	ADJUSTMENTS CREDIT	ADJUSTED TRIAL BALANCE DEBIT	ADJUSTED TRIAL BALANCE CREDIT	INCOME STATEMENT DEBIT	INCOME STATEMENT CREDIT	BALANCE SHEET DEBIT	BALANCE SHEET CREDIT
Cash	39,810.00				39,810.00				39,810.00	
Accounts Receivable	32,340.00				32,340.00				32,340.00	
Allowance for Doubtful Accounts		5,060.00		2,900.00		7,960.00				7,960.00
Merchandise Inventory	116,780.00		109,250.00	116,780.00	109,250.00				109,250.00	
Supplies	10,600.00			7,820.00	2,780.00				2,780.00	
Store Equipment	84,000.00				84,000.00				84,000.00	
Accum. Depr., Store Equip.		16,590.00		8,100.00		24,690.00				24,690.00
Office Equipment	25,700.00				25,700.00				25,700.00	
Accum. Depr., Office Equip.		7,033.00		5,875.00		12,908.00				12,908.00
Accounts Payable		22,560.00				22,560.00				22,560.00
Salaries Payable				4,750.00		4,750.00				4,750.00
Social Security Tax Payable				294.50		294.50				294.50
Medicare Tax Payable				68.88		68.88				68.88
Pietro Canzone, Capital		230,764.00				230,764.00				230,764.00
Pietro Canzone, Drawing	26,000.00				26,000.00				26,000.00	
Income Summary			116,780.00	109,250.00	116,780.00	109,250.00	116,780.00	109,250.00		
Sales		424,642.00				424,642.00		424,642.00		
Sales Returns and Allowances	8,155.00				8,155.00		8,155.00			
Purchases	197,534.00				197,534.00		197,534.00			
Purchases Returns and Allowances		1,200.00				1,200.00		1,200.00		
Purchases Discounts		600.00				600.00		600.00		
Freight In	12,260.00				12,260.00		12,260.00			
Sales Salaries Expense	94,580.00		4,000.00		98,580.00		98,580.00			
Rent Expense	31,000.00				31,000.00		31,000.00			
Advertising Expense	12,045.00				12,045.00		12,045.00			
Supplies Expense			7,820.00		7,820.00		7,820.00			
Depreciation Exp., Store Equip.			8,100.00		8,100.00		8,100.00			
Office Salaries Expense	17,645.00		750.00		18,395.00		18,395.00			
Payroll Taxes Expense			363.38		363.38		363.38			
Depreciation Exp., Office Equip.			5,875.00		5,875.00		5,875.00			
Uncollectible Accounts Expense			2,900.00		2,900.00		2,900.00			
	708,449.00	708,449.00	255,838.38	255,838.38	839,687.38	839,687.38	519,807.38	535,692.00	319,880.00	303,995.38
Net income							15,884.62			15,884.62
							535,692.00	535,692.00	319,880.00	319,880.00

WORKING PAPERS

Name ____________________

EXERCISE 12.1

GENERAL JOURNAL PAGE ____

	DATE		DESCRIPTION	POST. REF.	DEBIT	CREDIT	
1							1
2							2
3							3
4							4
5							5
6							6
7							7

EXERCISE 12.2

____

____

____

EXERCISE 12.3

GENERAL JOURNAL PAGE ____

	DATE		DESCRIPTION	POST. REF.	DEBIT	CREDIT	
1							1
2							2
3							3
4							4
5							5
6							6
7							7
8							8
9							9
10							10
11							11
12							12
13							13
14							14
15							15
16							16
17							17
18							18

Name ____________________

EXERCISE 12.4

GENERAL JOURNAL

PAGE ______

DATE		DESCRIPTION	POST. REF.	DEBIT	CREDIT

EXERCISE 12.5

GENERAL JOURNAL

PAGE ______

DATE		DESCRIPTION	POST. REF.	DEBIT	CREDIT

EXERCISE 12.6

GENERAL JOURNAL

PAGE ______

DATE		DESCRIPTION	POST. REF.	DEBIT	CREDIT

Name ____________________

EXERCISE 12.7

GENERAL JOURNAL PAGE ______

	DATE		DESCRIPTION	POST. REF.	DEBIT	CREDIT	
1							1
2							2
3							3
4							4
5							5
6							6
7							7
8							8
9							9
10							10
11							11
12							12
13							13

Name

PROBLEM 12.1A or 12.1B

GENERAL JOURNAL

PAGE

DATE		DESCRIPTION	POST. REF.	DEBIT	CREDIT

Name

PROBLEM 12.1A or 12.1B (continued)

GENERAL JOURNAL

PAGE

DATE	DESCRIPTION	POST. REF.	DEBIT	CREDIT

Analyze:

Name

PROBLEM 12.2A or 12.2B

GENERAL JOURNAL

PAGE 1

DATE		DESCRIPTION	POST. REF.	DEBIT	CREDIT

Name

PROBLEM 12.2A or 12.2B (continued)

GENERAL JOURNAL PAGE 2

DATE		DESCRIPTION	POST. REF.	DEBIT	CREDIT

Analyze:

Name

PROBLEM 12.3A or 12.3B

ACCOUNT NAME	TRIAL BALANCE		ADJUSTMENTS	
	DEBIT	CREDIT	DEBIT	CREDIT

Name

PROBLEM 12.3A or 12.3B (continued)

ADJUSTED TRIAL BALANCE		INCOME STATEMENT		BALANCE SHEET		
DEBIT	CREDIT	DEBIT	CREDIT	DEBIT	CREDIT	
						1
						2
						3
						4
						5
						6
						7
						8
						9
						10
						11
						12
						13
						14
						15
						16
						17
						18
						19
						20
						21
						22
						23
						24
						25
						26
						27
						28
						29
						30
						31
						32

Analyze:

Name

PROBLEM 12.4A or 12.4B

ACCOUNT NAME	TRIAL BALANCE		ADJUSTMENTS	
	DEBIT	CREDIT	DEBIT	CREDIT

Name

PROBLEM 12.4A or 12.4B (continued)

ADJUSTED TRIAL BALANCE		INCOME STATEMENT		BALANCE SHEET		
DEBIT	CREDIT	DEBIT	CREDIT	DEBIT	CREDIT	
						1
						2
						3
						4
						5
						6
						7
						8
						9
						10
						11
						12
						13
						14
						15
						16
						17
						18
						19
						20
						21
						22
						23
						24
						25
						26
						27
						28
						29
						30
						31
						32
						33
						34

Name

PROBLEM 12.4A or 12.4B (continued)

	ACCOUNT NAME	TRIAL BALANCE		ADJUSTMENTS	
		DEBIT	CREDIT	DEBIT	CREDIT
1					
2					
3					
4					
5					
6					
7					
8					
9					
10					
11					
12					
13					
14					
15					
16					
17					
18					
19					
20					
21					
22					
23					
24					
25					
26					
27					
28					
29					
30					
31					
32					

Name

PROBLEM 12.4A or 12.4B (continued)

ADJUSTED TRIAL BALANCE		INCOME STATEMENT		BALANCE SHEET		
DEBIT	CREDIT	DEBIT	CREDIT	DEBIT	CREDIT	
						1
						2
						3
						4
						5
						6
						7
						8
						9
						10
						11
						12
						13
						14
						15
						16
						17
						18
						19
						20
						21
						22
						23
						24
						25
						26
						27
						28
						29
						30
						31
						32

Analyze:

Name ______________________

PROBLEM 12.5A or 12.5B

	ACCOUNT NAME	TRIAL BALANCE		ADJUSTMENTS	
		DEBIT	CREDIT	DEBIT	CREDIT
1					
2					
3					
4					
5					
6					
7					
8					
9					
10					
11					
12					
13					
14					
15					
16					
17					
18					
19					
20					
21					
22					
23					
24					
25					
26					
27					
28					
29					
30					
31					
32					
33					
34					

Name

PROBLEM 12.5A or 12.5B (continued)

ADJUSTED TRIAL BALANCE		INCOME STATEMENT		BALANCE SHEET		
DEBIT	CREDIT	DEBIT	CREDIT	DEBIT	CREDIT	
						1
						2
						3
						4
						5
						6
						7
						8
						9
						10
						11
						12
						13
						14
						15
						16
						17
						18
						19
						20
						21
						22
						23
						24
						25
						26
						27
						28
						29
						30
						31
						32
						33
						34

Name

PROBLEM 12.5A or 12.5B (continued)

	ACCOUNT NAME	TRIAL BALANCE		ADJUSTMENTS	
		DEBIT	CREDIT	DEBIT	CREDIT
1					
2					
3					
4					
5					
6					
7					
8					
9					
10					
11					
12					
13					
14					
15					
16					
17					
18					
19					
20					
21					
22					
23					
24					
25					
26					
27					
28					
29					
30					
31					
32					

Name

PROBLEM 12.5A or 12.5B (continued)

ADJUSTED TRIAL BALANCE		INCOME STATEMENT		BALANCE SHEET	
DEBIT	CREDIT	DEBIT	CREDIT	DEBIT	CREDIT

Analyze:

Name

PROBLEM 12.6A or 12.6B

ACCOUNT NAME	TRIAL BALANCE		ADJUSTMENTS	
	DEBIT	CREDIT	DEBIT	CREDIT

Name

PROBLEM 12.6A or 12.6B (continued)

ADJUSTED TRIAL BALANCE		INCOME STATEMENT		BALANCE SHEET	
DEBIT	CREDIT	DEBIT	CREDIT	DEBIT	CREDIT

Name ______________________

CRITICAL THINKING PROBLEM 12.1

ACCOUNT NAME	TRIAL BALANCE		ADJUSTMENTS	
	DEBIT	CREDIT	DEBIT	CREDIT

Name

CRITICAL THINKING PROBLEM 12.1 (continued)

ADJUSTED TRIAL BALANCE		INCOME STATEMENT		BALANCE SHEET		
DEBIT	CREDIT	DEBIT	CREDIT	DEBIT	CREDIT	
						1
						2
						3
						4
						5
						6
						7
						8
						9
						10
						11
						12
						13
						14
						15
						16
						17
						18
						19
						20
						21
						22
						23
						24
						25
						26
						27
						28
						29
						30
						31
						32
						33

Name

CRITICAL THINKING PROBLEM 12.1 (continued)

	ACCOUNT NAME	TRIAL BALANCE		ADJUSTMENTS	
		DEBIT	CREDIT	DEBIT	CREDIT
1					
2					
3					
4					
5					
6					
7					
8					
9					
10					
11					
12					
13					
14					
15					
16					
17					
18					
19					
20					
21					
22					
23					
24					
25					
26					
27					
28					
29					
30					
31					
32					

Name ______________________________

CRITICAL THINKING PROBLEM 12.1 (continued)

ADJUSTED TRIAL BALANCE		INCOME STATEMENT		BALANCE SHEET		
DEBIT	CREDIT	DEBIT	CREDIT	DEBIT	CREDIT	
						1
						2
						3
						4
						5
						6
						7
						8
						9
						10
						11
						12
						13
						14
						15
						16
						17
						18
						19
						20
						21
						22
						23
						24
						25
						26
						27
						28
						29
						30
						31
						32

Name

CRITICAL THINKING PROBLEM 12.1 (continued)

GENERAL JOURNAL PAGE 30

DATE		DESCRIPTION	POST. REF.	DEBIT	CREDIT

Name

CRITICAL THINKING PROBLEM 12.1 (continued)

GENERAL JOURNAL PAGE 32

DATE		DESCRIPTION	POST. REF.	DEBIT	CREDIT

Name

CRITICAL THINKING PROBLEM 12.1 (continued)

a. Net Sales

b. Net Delivered Cost of Purchases

c. Cost of Goods Sold

d. Net Income (from worksheet)

e. Capital, December 31

Analyze:

Name ____________________

CRITICAL THINKING PROBLEM 12.2

1. ____________________

2. ____________________

Name ______________________________

Chapter 12 Practice Test Answer Key

Part A True-False

1. T
2. T
3. T
4. F
5. F
6. F
7. F
8. T
9. T
10. T
11. T
12. F
13. T
14. T
15. F
16. F
17. F
18. T
19. T
20. F
21. T
22. T
23. F
24. T
25. T

Part B Exercises

GENERAL JOURNAL

PAGE 16

DATE		DESCRIPTION	POST. REF.	DEBIT	CREDIT
		Adjusting Entries			
2016		(Adjustment 1)			
Dec.	31	Supplies Expense		1 4 0 0 00	
		Store Supplies			1 4 0 0 00
		(Adjustment 2)			
	31	Interest Expense		2 5 00	
		Interest Payable			2 5 00
		(Adjustment 3)			
	31	Interest Receivable		7 0 00	
		Interest Income			7 0 00
		(Adjustment 4)			
	31	Insurance Expense		1 4 0 0 00	
		Prepaid Insurance			1 4 0 0 00
		(Adjustment 5)			
	31	Unearned Season Tickets Income		4 8 0 0 0 0 00	
		Season Tickets Income			4 8 0 0 0 0 00

CHAPTER 13

Financial Statements and Closing Procedures

STUDY GUIDE

Understanding the Chapter

Objectives

1. Prepare a classified income statement from the worksheet. **2.** Prepare a statement of owner's equity from the worksheet. **3.** Prepare a classified balance sheet from the worksheet. **4.** Journalize and post the adjusting entries. **5.** Journalize and post the closing entries. **6.** Prepare a postclosing trial balance. **7.** Journalize and post reversing entries. **8.** Define the accounting terms new to this chapter.

Reading Assignment

Read Chapter 13 in the textbook. Complete the textbook Section Self Review as you finish reading each section of the chapter, and the Comprehensive Self Review at the end of the chapter. Refer to the Chapter 13 Glossary or to the Glossary at the end of the book to find definitions for terms that are not familiar to you.

Activities

❑ **Thinking Critically** — Answer the *Thinking Critically* questions for Whole Foods Market and Managerial Implications.

❑ **Discussion Questions** — Answer each assigned discussion question in Chapter 13.

❑ **Exercises** — Complete each assigned exercise in Chapter 13. Use the forms provided in this SGWP. The objectives covered by an exercise are given after the exercise number. If you need help with an exercise, review the portion of the chapter related to the objective(s) covered.

❑ **Problems A/B** — Complete each assigned problem in Chapter 13. Use the forms provided in this SGWP. The objectives covered by a problem are given after the problem number. If you need help with a problem, review the portion of the chapter related to the objective(s) covered.

❑ **Critical Thinking Problems** — Complete the critical thinking problems as assigned. Use the forms provided in this SGWP.

❑ **Business Connections** — Complete the Business Connections activities as assigned to gain a deeper understanding of Chapter 13 concepts.

Practice Tests

Complete the Practice Tests, which cover the main points in your reading assignment. Compare your answers with those in the Practice Test Answer Key for Chapter 13 at the end of this chapter. If you have answered any questions incorrectly, review the related section of text.

STUDY GUIDE

Part A True-False *True-False For each of the following statements, circle T in the answer column if the statement is true or F if the statement is false.*

T F **1.** A company reported net sales of $2,000,000 and cost of goods sold of $1,200,000. The gross profit percentage is 60%.

T F **2.** Some accounts adjusted in the Adjustment columns of the worksheet do not require a reversing entry.

T F **3.** Cash, accounts receivable, merchandise inventory, and equipment are classified as current assets.

T F **4.** **Interest Payable** and **Depreciation Expense** are typical of accounts that do not require reversing entries.

T F **5.** Reversing entries are not required, but are highly recommended in order to improve efficiency and reduce errors.

T F **6.** In closing the **Income Summary** account, the net income or loss is closed into the owner's capital account.

T F **7.** **Income Summary** is credited for the total of the expenses and the beginning inventory.

T F **8.** Closing journal entries for December 31, 2016 should be reversed on January 1, 2017.

T F **9.** The ending merchandise inventory is recorded in the accounting records by an adjusting entry.

T F **10.** Adjustments are posted from the worksheet to the general ledger accounts.

T F **11.** The depreciation expense for the store equipment appears in the Plant and Equipment section of the classified balance sheet.

T F **12.** The net income or loss from operations shown on the classified income statement is the difference between gross profit on sales and total operating expenses.

T F **13.** The Cost of Goods Sold section of the classified income statement includes information about the beginning and ending merchandise inventory and the purchases and net sales made during the year.

T F **14.** The gross profit on sales shown on the classified income statement is the difference between the net sales and the operating expenses.

T F **15.** Current liabilities are debts that are due for payment after one year from the balance sheet date.

T F **16.** Short-term notes receivable, cash, accounts receivable, merchandise inventory and prepaid expense items appear in the Current Assets section of the classified balance sheet.

T F **17.** The postclosing trial balance shows essentially the same account balances that appear in the balance sheet.

T F **18.** It is desirable to prepare a postclosing trial balance after the adjusting and closing entries have been journalized and posted.

T F **19.** The **Income Summary** account is closed at the end of the period.

T F 20. Asset, liability, and owner's capital accounts are the only accounts carried forward from one year to the next.

T F 21. The information needed to close the revenue and expense accounts is taken directly from the ledger accounts to ensure accuracy.

T F 22. The revenue and expense accounts are the only accounts carried forward from one year to the next.

T F 23. After completing the worksheet and the financial statements, adjustments are entered in the general journal.

T F 24. After all adjustments have been journalized and posted, the ledger account balances should be the same as the postclosing trial balance amounts.

T F 25. The drawing account is closed into the **Income Summary** account as one of the last closing entries.

Demonstration Problem

A partial worksheet showing the end-of-year operating results for Extreme Sports for 2016 follows.

Instructions

1. Prepare a classified income statement. Sports Warehouse does not classify its operating expenses as selling and administrative expenses.
2. Prepare a statement of owner's equity. No additional investments were made during the period.
3. Prepare a classified balance sheet as of December 31, 2016. All notes payable are due within one year.
4. Journalize the closing entries on page 45 of the general journal.
5. Compute the gross profit percentage for the year ended December 31, 2016. Round your answer to one decimal.
6. Compute the current ratio at December 31, 2016. Round your answer to two decimal places.
7. Compute the inventory turnover ratio for the year ended December 31, 2016. Round your answer to two decimal places.
8. Compute the accounts receivable turnover for the year ended December 31, 2016. The net accounts receivable balance at December 31, 2015 was $59,340. Round your answer to two decimal places.

DEMONSTRATION PROBLEM (continued)

Extreme Sports
Worksheet (Partial)
Year Ended December 31, 2016

	ACCOUNT NAME	INCOME STATEMENT DEBIT	INCOME STATEMENT CREDIT	BALANCE SHEET DEBIT	BALANCE SHEET CREDIT
1	Cash			25,285.00	
2	Accounts Receivable			61,258.00	
3	Allowance for Doubtful Accounts				5,930.00
4	Merchandise Inventory			197,214.00	
5	Supplies			3,512.00	
6	Prepaid Insurance			37,000.00	
7	Equipment			83,290.00	
8	Accumulated Depreciation—Equipment				24,330.00
9	Notes Payable				47,500.00
10	Accounts Payable				44,860.00
11	Social Security Tax Payable				2,683.00
12	Medicare Tax Payable				845.00
13	Salaries Payable				7,530.00
14	Interest Payable				3,660.00
15	Raul Flores, Capital				260,730.00
16	Raul Flores, Drawing			50,000.00	
17	Income Summary	201,345.00	197,214.00		
18	Sales		627,690.00		
19	Sales Returns and Allowances	11,950.00			
20	Purchases	280,174.00			
21	Purchases Returns and Allowances		10,440.00		
22	Freight In	11,410.00			
23	Purchases Discounts		11,921.00		
24	Telephone Expense	4,171.00			
25	Salaries Expense	241,380.00			
26	Payroll Tax Expense	13,104.00			
27	Supplies Expense	6,060.00			
28	Insurance Expense	5,000.00			
29	Depreciation Expense—Equipment	7,420.00			
30	Uncollectible Accounts Expense	2,600.00			
31	Interest Expense	3,160.00			
32	Totals	787,774.00	847,265.00	457,559.00	398,068.00
33	Net Income	59,491.00			59,491.00
34		847,265.00	847,265.00	457,559.00	457,559.00
35					

SOLUTION

(1.)

Extreme Sports
Income Statement
Year Ended December 31, 2016

Operating Revenue				
Sales				627,690.00
Less Sales Returns and Allowances				11,950.00
Net Sales				615,740.00
Cost of Goods Sold				
Merchandise Inventory, Jan. 1, 2016			201,345.00	
Purchases		280,174.00		
Freight In		11,410.00		
Delivered Cost of Purchases		291,584.00		
Less Purchase Returns and Allow.	10,440.00			
Purchase Discounts	11,921.00	22,361.00		
Net Delivered Cost of Purchases			269,223.00	
Total Merchandise Available for Sale			470,568.00	
Less Merchandise Inv., Dec. 31, 2016			197,214.00	
Cost of Goods Sold				273,354.00
Gross Profit on Sales				342,386.00
Operating Expenses				
Telephone Expense			4,171.00	
Salaries Expense			241,380.00	
Payroll Tax Expense			13,104.00	
Supplies Expense			6,060.00	
Insurance Expense			5,000.00	
Depreciation Expense—Equipment			7,420.00	
Uncollectible Accounts Expense			2,600.00	
Total Operating Expenses				279,735.00
Income from Operations				62,651.00
Other Expenses				
Interest Expense				3,160.00
Net Income for Year				59,491.00

SOLUTION (continued)

(2.)

Extreme Sports
Statement of Owner's Equity
Year Ended December 31, 2016

Raul Flores, Capital, Jan. 1, 2016			260,730.00
Net Income for Year		59,491.00	
Less Withdrawals for the Year		50,000.00	
Increase in Capital			9,491.00
Raul Flores, Capital, Dec. 31, 2016			270,221.00

(3.)

Extreme Sports
Balance Sheet
December 31, 2016

Assets			
Current Assets			
Cash			25,285.00
Accounts Receivable		61,258.00	
Less Allowance for Doubtful Accounts		5,930.00	55,328.00
Merchandise Inventory			197,214.00
Prepaid Expenses			
Supplies		3,512.00	
Prepaid Insurance		37,000.00	40,512.00
Total Current Assets			318,339.00
Plant and Equipment			
Equipment		83,290.00	
Less Accumulated Depreciation		24,330.00	
Total Plant and Equipment			58,960.00
Total Assets			377,299.00
Liabilities and Owner's Equity			
Current Liabilities			
Notes Payable		47,500.00	
Accounts Payable		44,860.00	
Interest Payable		3,660.00	
Social Security Tax Payable		2,683.00	
Medicare Tax Payable		845.00	
Salaries Payable		7,530.00	
Total Current Liabilities			107,078.00
Owner's Equity			
Raul Flores, Capital			270,221.00
Total Liabilities and Owner's Equity			377,299.00

SOLUTION (continued)

(4.)

GENERAL JOURNAL

PAGE 45

DATE		DESCRIPTION	POST. REF.	DEBIT	CREDIT
		Closing Entries			
2016					
Dec.	**31**	**Sales**		627,690.00	
		Purchase Returns and Allowances		10,440.00	
		Purchases Discounts		11,921.00	
		Income Summary			650,051.00
	31	**Income Summary**		586,429.00	
		Sales Returns and Allowances			11,950.00
		Purchases			280,174.00
		Freight In			11,410.00
		Telephone Expense			4,171.00
		Salaries Expense			241,380.00
		Payroll Taxes Expense			13,104.00
		Supplies Expense			6,060.00
		Insurance Expense			5,000.00
		Depreciation Expense—Equipment			7,420.00
		Uncollectible Accounts Expense			2,600.00
		Interest Expense			3,160.00
	31	**Income Summary**		59,491.00	
		Raul Flores, Capital			59,491.00
	31	**Raul Flores, Capital**		50,000.00	
		Raul Flores, Drawing			50,000.00

(5.) The gross profit percentage for the year ended December 31, 2016 is 55.6% ($342,386/$615,740).

(6.) The current ratio at December 31, 2016 is 2.97 ($318,339/$107,078).

(7.) The inventory turnover ratio for the year ended December 31, 2016 is 1.37 ($273,354/$199,279.50).

(8.) The accounts receivable turnover ratio for the year ended December 31, 2016 is 10.74 ($615,740/$57,334).

WORKING PAPERS

Name ______________________

EXERCISE 13.1

1. Purchases Returns and Allowances ______
2. Telephone Expense ______
3. Sales Returns and Allowances ______
4. Purchases ______
5. Interest Income ______
6. Merchandise Inventory ______
7. Interest Expense ______
8. Sales ______
9. Depreciation Expense—Store Equipment ______
10. Rent Expense ______

EXERCISE 13.2x

1. Accounts Receivable ______
2. Delivery Van ______
3. Prepaid Insurance ______
4. Notes Payable, due 2014 ______
5. Store Supplies ______
6. Accounts Payable ______
7. Merchandise Inventory ______
8. Ray Lynch, Capital ______
9. Cash ______
10. Unearned Subscription Income ______

EXERCISE 13.3

(continued)

Name

EXERCISE 13.3 (continued)

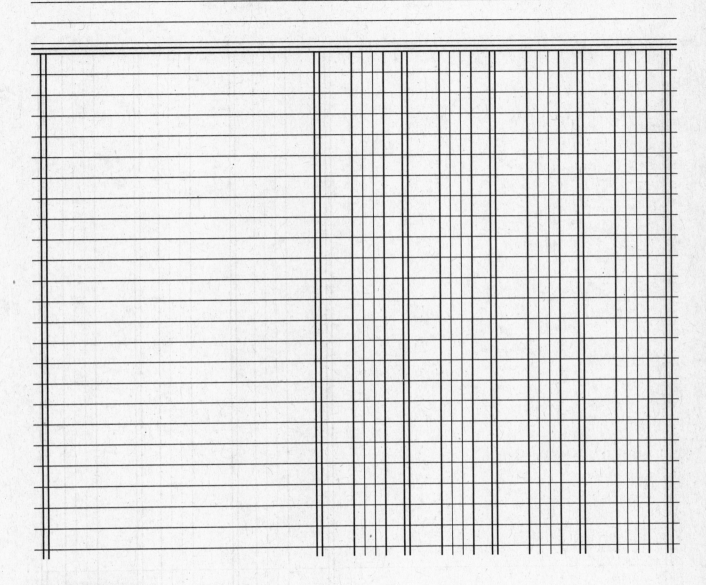

EXERCISE 13.4

Name

EXERCISE 13.5

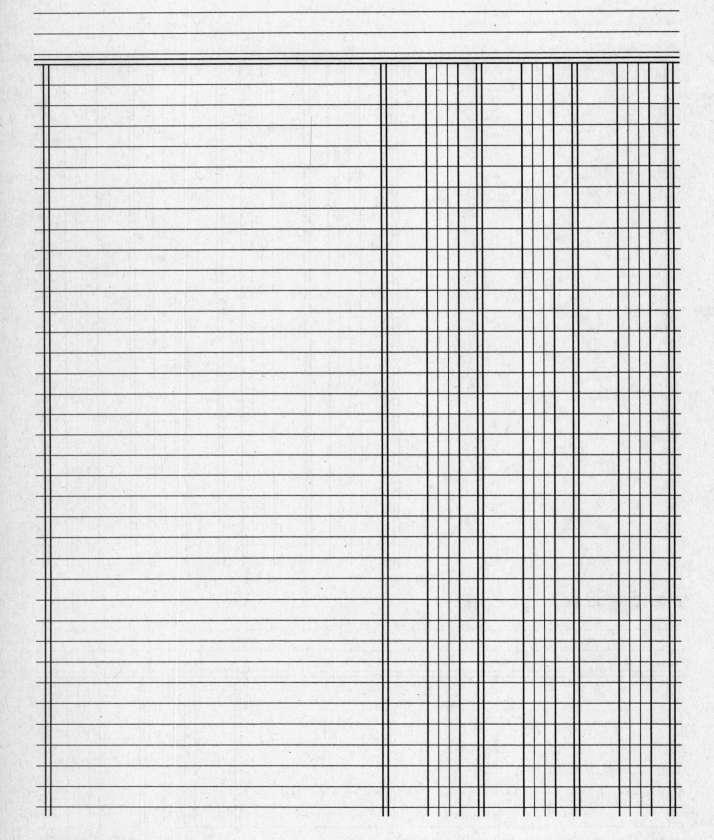

Name ______________________

EXERCISE 13.6

GENERAL JOURNAL

PAGE ______

DATE	DESCRIPTION	POST. REF.	DEBIT	CREDIT

Name

EXERCISE 13.7

GENERAL JOURNAL

PAGE

DATE		DESCRIPTION	POST. REF.	DEBIT	CREDIT

Name

EXERCISE 13.8

ACCOUNT NAME	DEBIT	CREDIT

Name ______________________

EXERCISE 13.9

a. Net Sales is

Gross profit is

The gross profit percentage is

b. Current assets are

Current liabilities are

Working capital is

Name ______________________

EXERCISE 13.9 (continued)

c. The current ratio is ______________________

d. The inventory turnover is ______________________

EXERCISE 13.10

a.

b.

Name

PROBLEM 13.1A or 13.1B

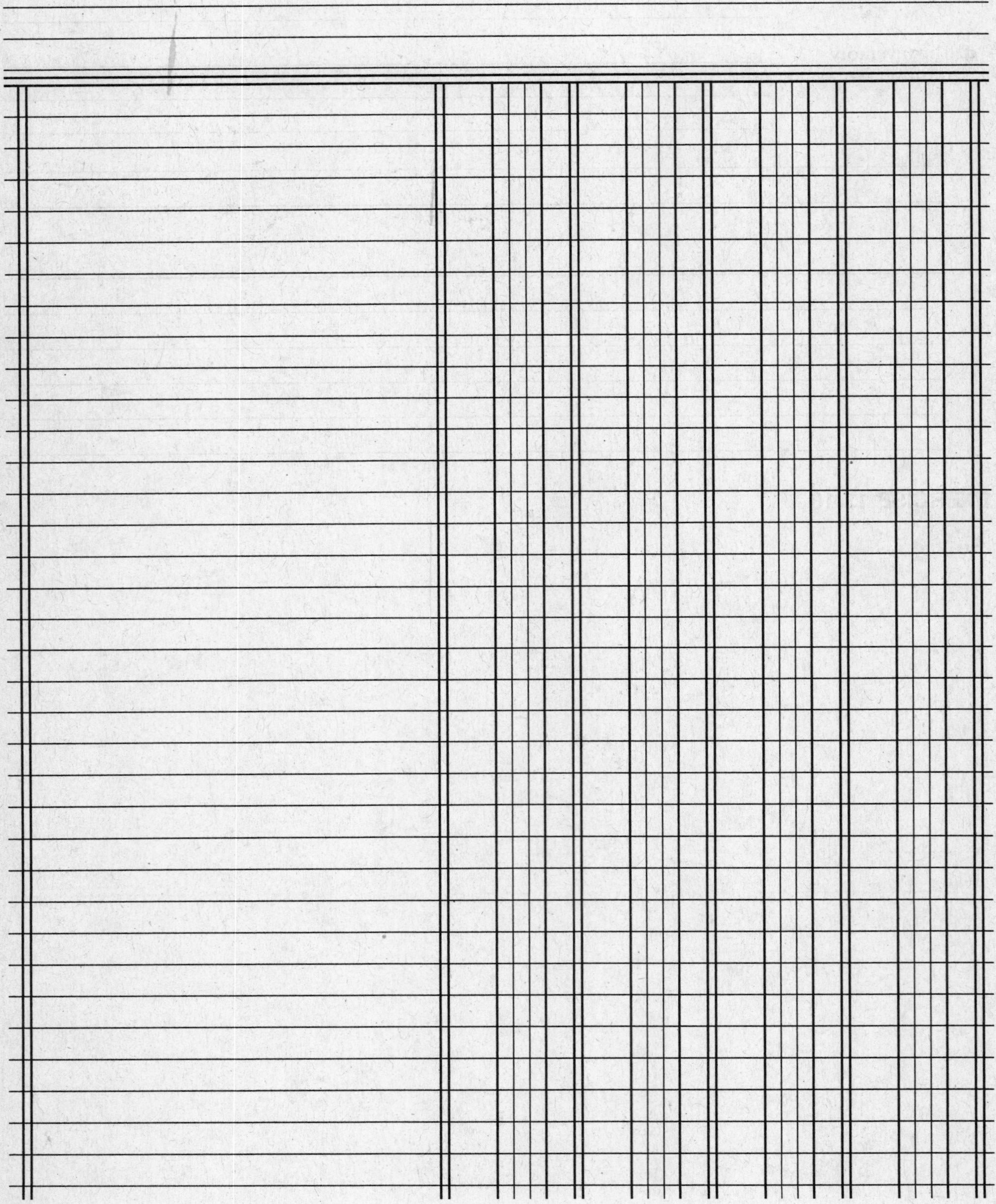

(continued)

Name

PROBLEM 13.1A or 13.1B (continued)

Name

PROBLEM 13.1A or 13.1B (continued)

(continued)

Name

PROBLEM 13.1A or 13.1B (continued)

Analyze:

Name

PROBLEM 13.2A or 13.2B

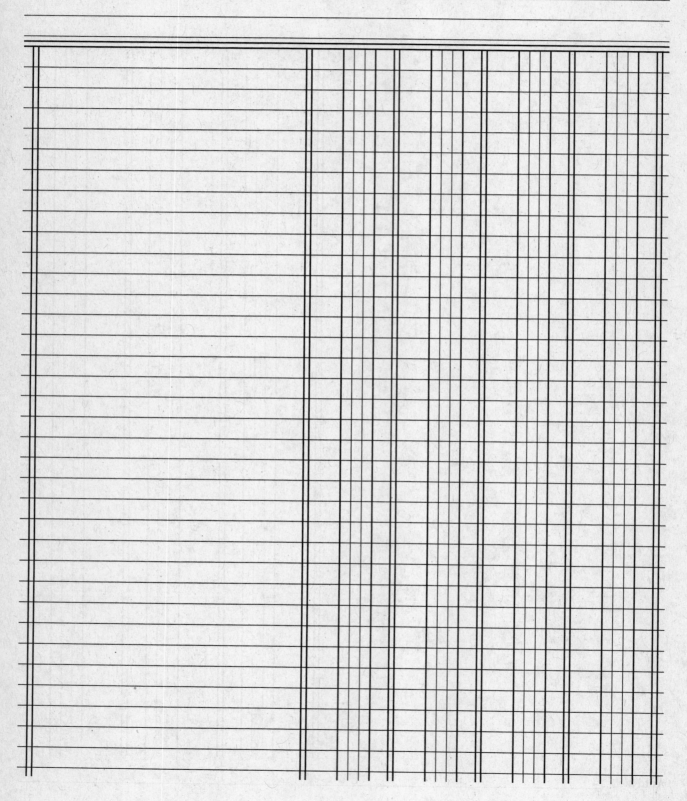

(continued)

Name

PROBLEM 13.2A or 13.2B (continued)

Name

PROBLEM 13.2A or 13.2B (continued)

(continued)

Name

PROBLEM 13.2A or 13.2B (continued)

Analyze:

Name

PROBLEM 13.3A or 13.3B

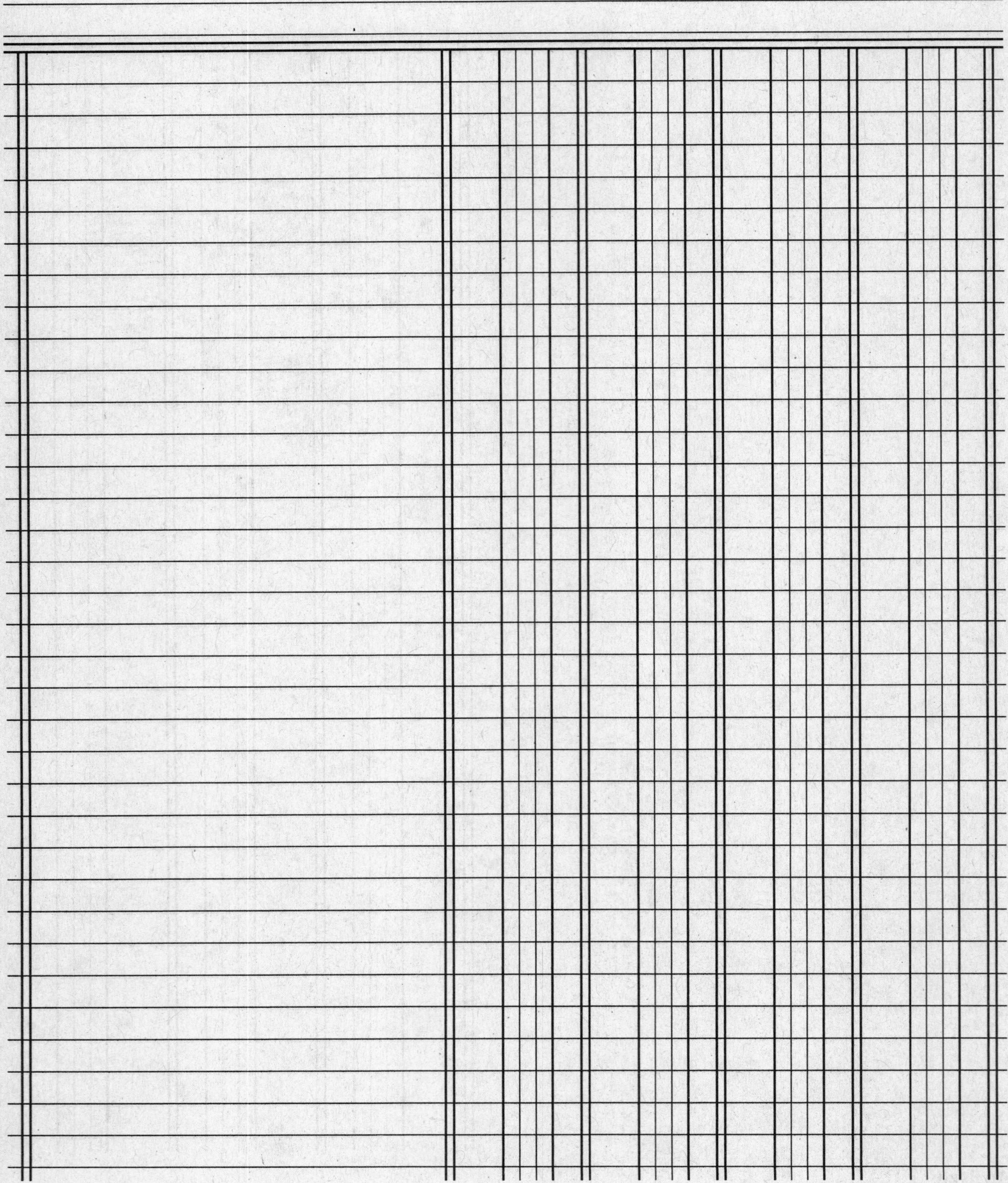

(continued)

Name

PROBLEM 13.3A or 13.3B (continued)

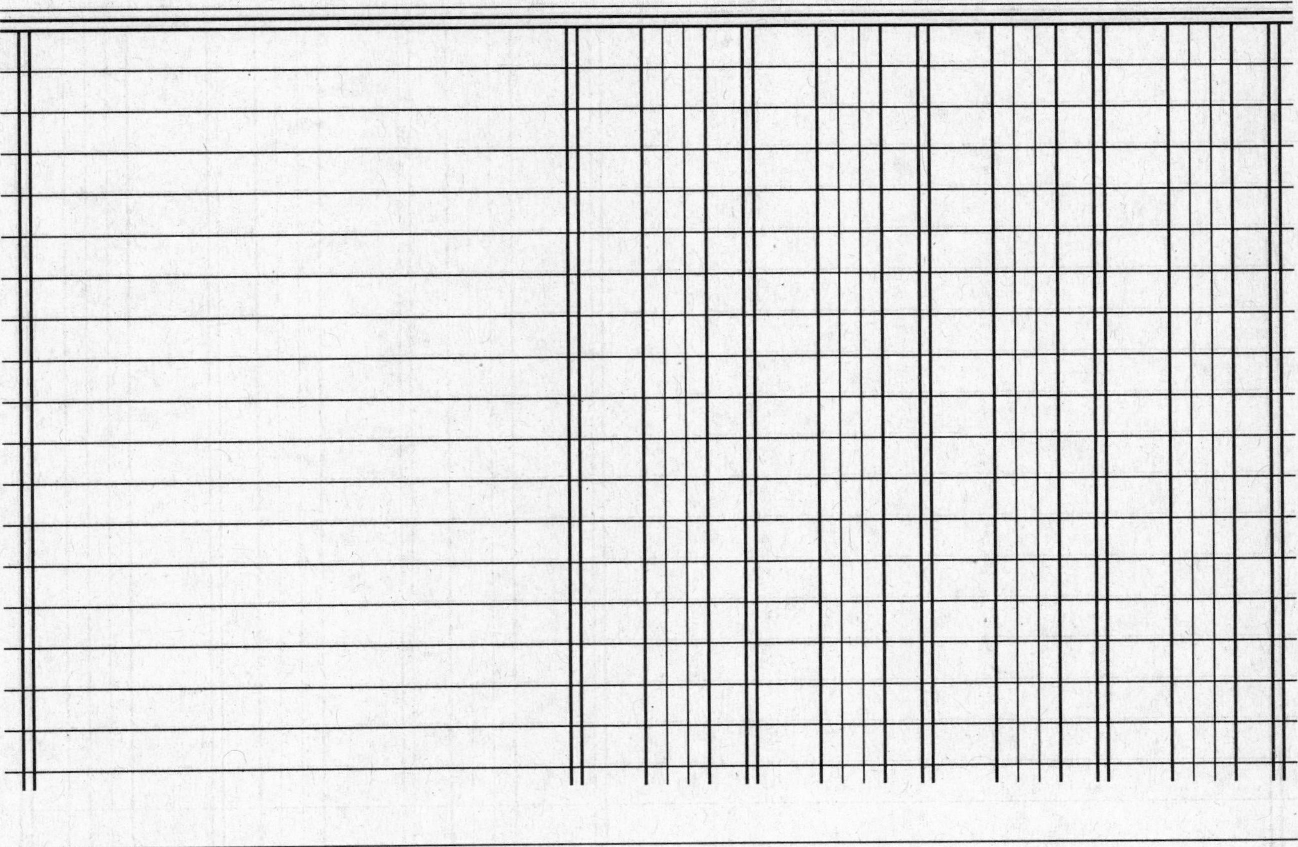

Name

PROBLEM 13.3A or 13.3B (continued)

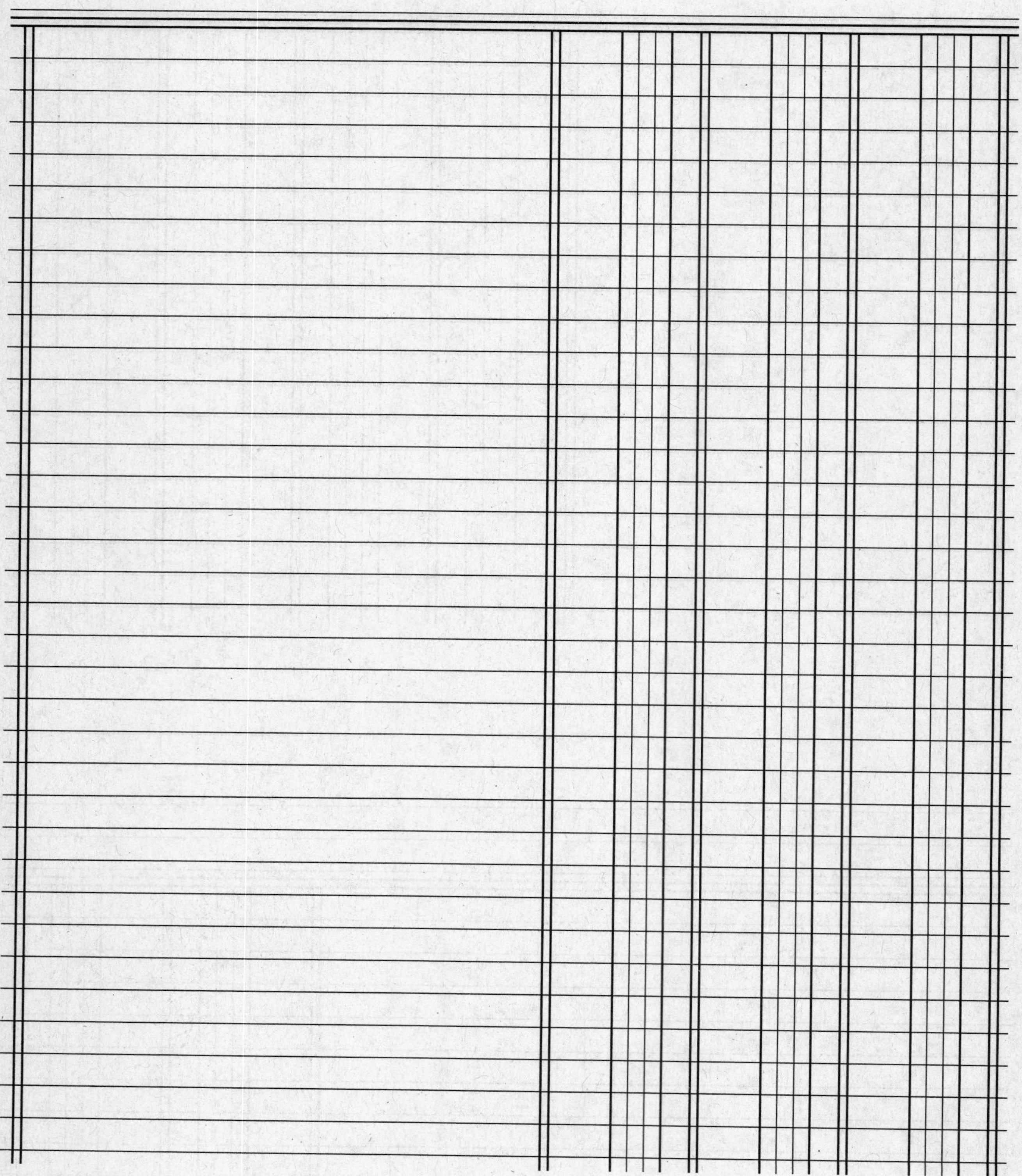

(continued)

Name

PROBLEM 13.3A or 13.3B (continued)

Analyze:

Name

PROBLEM 13.4A or 13.4B

GENERAL JOURNAL

PAGE

DATE		DESCRIPTION	POST. REF.	DEBIT	CREDIT

Name

PROBLEM 13.4A or 13.4B (continued)

GENERAL JOURNAL

PAGE

DATE	DESCRIPTION	POST. REF.	DEBIT	CREDIT

Name ______________________

PROBLEM 13.4A or 13.4B (continued)

GENERAL JOURNAL

PAGE ______

DATE	DESCRIPTION	POST. REF.	DEBIT	CREDIT

Name ______________________

PROBLEM 13.4A or 13.4B (continued)

GENERAL JOURNAL

PAGE ______

	DATE		DESCRIPTION	POST. REF.	DEBIT	CREDIT	
1							1
2							2
3							3
4							4
5							5
6							6
7							7
8							8
9							9
10							10
11							11
12							12
13							13
14							14
15							15
16							16
17							17
18							18
19							19
20							20
21							21
22							22
23							23
24							24
25							25

Analyze: ____

PAGE ______

	DATE		DESCRIPTION	POST. REF.	DEBIT	CREDIT	
1							1
2							2
3							3
4							4
5							5
6							6

Name

PROBLEM 13.5A or 13.5B

GENERAL JOURNAL

PAGE

DATE		DESCRIPTION	POST. REF.	DEBIT	CREDIT

Name ______________________

PROBLEM 13.5A or 13.5B (continued)

GENERAL JOURNAL PAGE ______

	DATE		DESCRIPTION	POST. REF.	DEBIT	CREDIT	
1							1
2							2
3							3
4							4
5							5
6							6
7							7
8							8
9							9
10							10
11							11
12							12
13							13
14							14
15							15
16							16

Analyze: ______________________

EXTRA FORM

GENERAL JOURNAL PAGE ______

	DATE		DESCRIPTION	POST. REF.	DEBIT	CREDIT	
1							1
2							2
3							3
4							4
5							5
6							6
7							7
8							8
9							9
10							10
11							11
12							12
13							13

Name

CRITICAL THINKING PROBLEM 13.1

ACCOUNT NAME	TRIAL BALANCE		ADJUSTMENTS	
	DEBIT	CREDIT	DEBIT	CREDIT

Name ______________________

CRITICAL THINKING PROBLEM 13.1 (continued)

ADJUSTED TRIAL BALANCE		INCOME STATEMENT		BALANCE SHEET		
DEBIT	CREDIT	DEBIT	CREDIT	DEBIT	CREDIT	
						1
						2
						3
						4
						5
						6
						7
						8
						9
						10
						11
						12
						13
						14
						15
						16
						17
						18
						19
						20
						21
						22
						23
						24
						25
						26
						27
						28
						29
						30
						31
						32
						33
						34
						35
						36

Name ______________________

CRITICAL THINKING PROBLEM 13.1 (continued)

Name

CRITICAL THINKING PROBLEM 13.1 (continued)

EXTRA FORM

Name

CRITICAL THINKING PROBLEM 13.1 (continued)

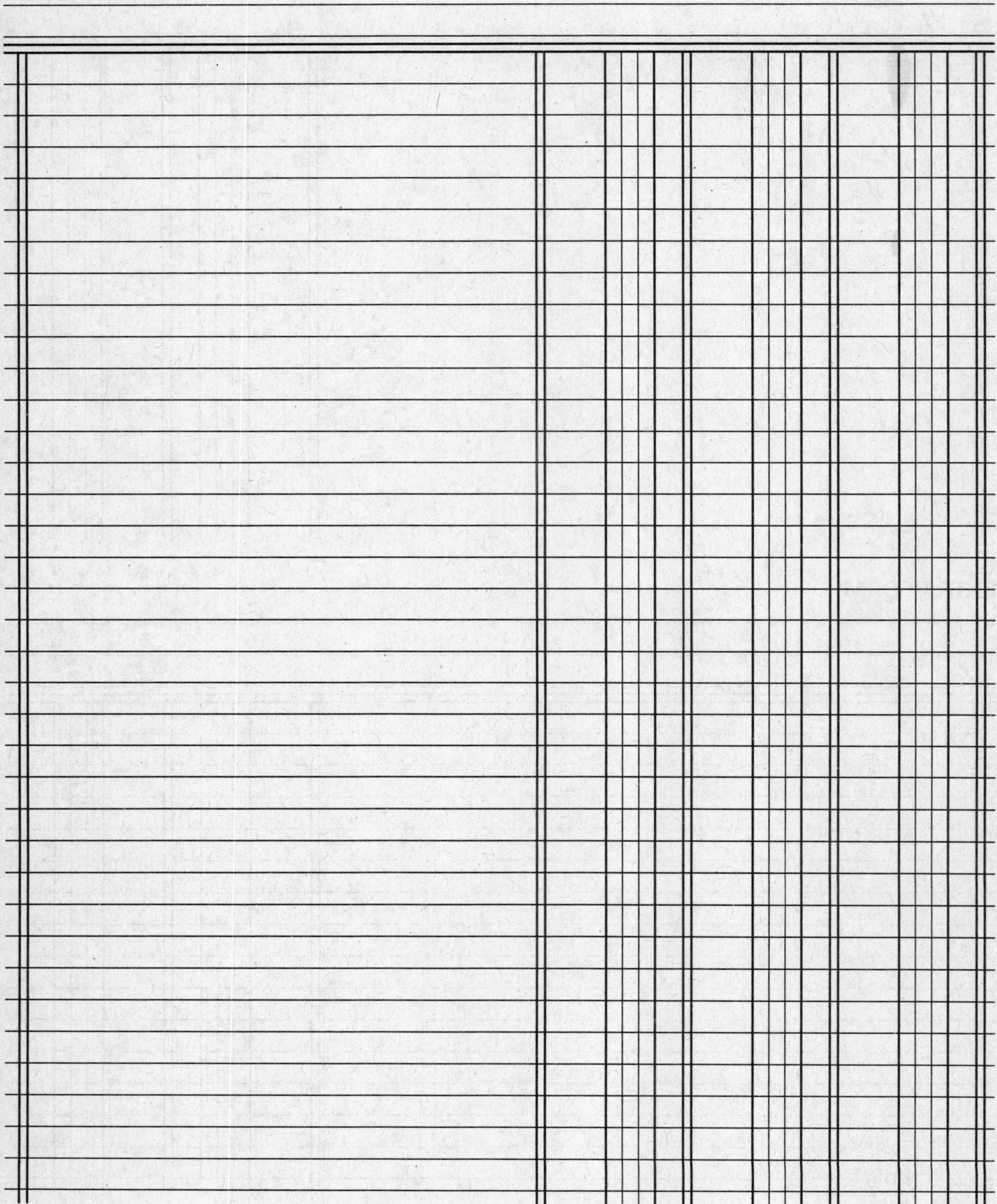

Name

CRITICAL THINKING PROBLEM 13.1 (continued)

GENERAL JOURNAL PAGE

DATE	DESCRIPTION	POST. REF.	DEBIT	CREDIT

Name ______________________

CRITICAL THINKING PROBLEM 13.1 (continued)

GENERAL JOURNAL PAGE ______

	DATE		DESCRIPTION	POST. REF.	DEBIT	CREDIT	
1							1
2							2
3							3
4							4
5							5
6							6
7							7
8							8
9							9
10							10
11							11
12							12
13							13
14							14
15							15
16							16
17							17
18							18
19							19
20							20
21							21
22							22
23							23
24							24
25							25
26							26
27							27
28							28
29							29
30							30
31							31
32							32
33							33
34							34
35							35
36							36
37							37

Name ____________________

CRITICAL THINKING PROBLEM 13.1 (continued)

GENERAL JOURNAL PAGE ______

DATE		DESCRIPTION	POST. REF.	DEBIT	CREDIT

Name ____________________

CRITICAL THINKING PROBLEM 13.1 (continued)

GENERAL JOURNAL — PAGE ______

	DATE	DESCRIPTION	POST. REF.	DEBIT	CREDIT	
1						1
2						2
3						3
4						4
5						5
6						6
7						7
8						8
9						9
10						10
11						11
12						12
13						13
14						14
15						15
16						16
17						17
18						18
19						19
20						20
21						21
22						22
23						23
24						24
25						25
26						26
27						27
28						28
29						29
30						30
31						31
32						32
33						33
34						34

Analyze: ____________________

Name

CRITICAL THINKING PROBLEM 13.2

1.

2.

Name

CHAPTER 13 CRITICAL THINKING PROBLEM (continued)

3.

Chapter 13 Practice Test Answer Key

Part A True-False

1. F	6. T	11. F	16. T	21. F
2. T	7. F	12. T	17. T	22. F
3. F	8. F	13. F	18. T	23. T
4. F	9. T	14. F	19. T	24. T
5. T	10. F	15. F	20. T	25. F

MINI-PRACTICE SET 2

Merchandising Business Accounting Cycle

GENERAL JOURNAL

PAGE ______

DATE		DESCRIPTION	POST. REF.	DEBIT	CREDIT

Name ______________________

GENERAL JOURNAL

PAGE ________

DATE		DESCRIPTION	POST. REF.	DEBIT	CREDIT

MINI-PRACTICE SET 2 (continued)

Name ____________________

GENERAL JOURNAL

PAGE ________

DATE	DESCRIPTION	POST. REF.	DEBIT	CREDIT

 Name

GENERAL JOURNAL

PAGE

DATE		DESCRIPTION	POST. REF.	DEBIT	CREDIT

MINI-PRACTICE SET 2 (continued)

Name

GENERAL JOURNAL

PAGE

DATE		DESCRIPTION	POST. REF.	DEBIT	CREDIT

 Name

GENERAL JOURNAL

PAGE

DATE	DESCRIPTION	POST. REF.	DEBIT	CREDIT

Name ________________

GENERAL JOURNAL

PAGE ________

DATE	DESCRIPTION	POST. REF.	DEBIT	CREDIT

Name

GENERAL JOURNAL

PAGE

DATE	DESCRIPTION	POST. REF.	DEBIT	CREDIT

 Name

ACCOUNT ACCOUNT NO.

DATE	DESCRIPTION	POST. REF.	DEBIT	CREDIT	BALANCE	
					DEBIT	CREDIT

 Name

GENERAL LEDGER

ACCOUNT ACCOUNT NO.

DATE		DESCRIPTION	POST. REF.	DEBIT	CREDIT	BALANCE	
						DEBIT	CREDIT

ACCOUNT ACCOUNT NO.

DATE		DESCRIPTION	POST. REF.	DEBIT	CREDIT	BALANCE	
						DEBIT	CREDIT

ACCOUNT ACCOUNT NO.

DATE		DESCRIPTION	POST. REF.	DEBIT	CREDIT	BALANCE	
						DEBIT	CREDIT

 Name ____________

GENERAL LEDGER

ACCOUNT ____________ ACCOUNT NO. ______

DATE		DESCRIPTION	POST. REF.	DEBIT	CREDIT	BALANCE	
						DEBIT	CREDIT

ACCOUNT ____________ ACCOUNT NO. ______

DATE		DESCRIPTION	POST. REF.	DEBIT	CREDIT	BALANCE	
						DEBIT	CREDIT

ACCOUNT ____________ ACCOUNT NO. ______

DATE		DESCRIPTION	POST. REF.	DEBIT	CREDIT	BALANCE	
						DEBIT	CREDIT

ACCOUNT ____________ ACCOUNT NO. ______

DATE		DESCRIPTION	POST. REF.	DEBIT	CREDIT	BALANCE	
						DEBIT	CREDIT

 Name ______

GENERAL LEDGER

ACCOUNT ______ ACCOUNT NO. ______

DATE		DESCRIPTION	POST. REF.	DEBIT	CREDIT	BALANCE	
						DEBIT	CREDIT

ACCOUNT ______ ACCOUNT NO. ______

DATE		DESCRIPTION	POST. REF.	DEBIT	CREDIT	BALANCE	
						DEBIT	CREDIT

ACCOUNT ______ ACCOUNT NO. ______

DATE		DESCRIPTION	POST. REF.	DEBIT	CREDIT	BALANCE	
						DEBIT	CREDIT

Name

GENERAL LEDGER

ACCOUNT ACCOUNT NO.

DATE		DESCRIPTION	POST. REF.	DEBIT	CREDIT	BALANCE DEBIT	BALANCE CREDIT

ACCOUNT ACCOUNT NO.

DATE		DESCRIPTION	POST. REF.	DEBIT	CREDIT	BALANCE DEBIT	BALANCE CREDIT

ACCOUNT ACCOUNT NO.

DATE		DESCRIPTION	POST. REF.	DEBIT	CREDIT	BALANCE DEBIT	BALANCE CREDIT

ACCOUNT ACCOUNT NO.

DATE		DESCRIPTION	POST. REF.	DEBIT	CREDIT	BALANCE DEBIT	BALANCE CREDIT

 Name

GENERAL LEDGER

ACCOUNT ACCOUNT NO.

DATE		DESCRIPTION	POST. REF.	DEBIT	CREDIT	BALANCE	
						DEBIT	CREDIT

ACCOUNT ACCOUNT NO.

DATE		DESCRIPTION	POST. REF.	DEBIT	CREDIT	BALANCE	
						DEBIT	CREDIT

ACCOUNT ACCOUNT NO.

DATE		DESCRIPTION	POST. REF.	DEBIT	CREDIT	BALANCE	
						DEBIT	CREDIT

 Name ______

GENERAL LEDGER

ACCOUNT ______ ACCOUNT NO. ______

DATE		DESCRIPTION	POST. REF.	DEBIT	CREDIT	BALANCE DEBIT	BALANCE CREDIT

ACCOUNT ______ ACCOUNT NO. ______

DATE		DESCRIPTION	POST. REF.	DEBIT	CREDIT	BALANCE DEBIT	BALANCE CREDIT

ACCOUNT ______ ACCOUNT NO. ______

DATE		DESCRIPTION	POST. REF.	DEBIT	CREDIT	BALANCE DEBIT	BALANCE CREDIT

 Name

GENERAL LEDGER

ACCOUNT ______ ACCOUNT NO. ______

DATE		DESCRIPTION	POST. REF.	DEBIT	CREDIT	BALANCE	
						DEBIT	CREDIT

ACCOUNT ______ ACCOUNT NO. ______

DATE		DESCRIPTION	POST. REF.	DEBIT	CREDIT	BALANCE	
						DEBIT	CREDIT

ACCOUNT ______ ACCOUNT NO. ______

DATE		DESCRIPTION	POST. REF.	DEBIT	CREDIT	BALANCE	
						DEBIT	CREDIT

ACCOUNT ______ ACCOUNT NO. ______

DATE		DESCRIPTION	POST. REF.	DEBIT	CREDIT	BALANCE	
						DEBIT	CREDIT

 Name

GENERAL LEDGER

ACCOUNT ______ ACCOUNT NO. ______

DATE		DESCRIPTION	POST. REF.	DEBIT	CREDIT	BALANCE DEBIT	BALANCE CREDIT

ACCOUNT ______ ACCOUNT NO. ______

DATE		DESCRIPTION	POST. REF.	DEBIT	CREDIT	BALANCE DEBIT	BALANCE CREDIT

ACCOUNT ______ ACCOUNT NO. ______

DATE		DESCRIPTION	POST. REF.	DEBIT	CREDIT	BALANCE DEBIT	BALANCE CREDIT

ACCOUNT ______ ACCOUNT NO. ______

DATE		DESCRIPTION	POST. REF.	DEBIT	CREDIT	BALANCE DEBIT	BALANCE CREDIT

 Name

GENERAL LEDGER

ACCOUNT ACCOUNT NO.

DATE		DESCRIPTION	POST. REF.	DEBIT	CREDIT	BALANCE	
						DEBIT	CREDIT

ACCOUNT ACCOUNT NO.

DATE		DESCRIPTION	POST. REF.	DEBIT	CREDIT	BALANCE	
						DEBIT	CREDIT

ACCOUNT ACCOUNT NO.

DATE		DESCRIPTION	POST. REF.	DEBIT	CREDIT	BALANCE	
						DEBIT	CREDIT

ACCOUNT ACCOUNT NO.

DATE		DESCRIPTION	POST. REF.	DEBIT	CREDIT	BALANCE	
						DEBIT	CREDIT

ACCOUNT ACCOUNT NO.

DATE		DESCRIPTION	POST. REF.	DEBIT	CREDIT	BALANCE	
						DEBIT	CREDIT

Name

GENERAL LEDGER

ACCOUNT ACCOUNT NO.

DATE		DESCRIPTION	POST. REF.	DEBIT	CREDIT	BALANCE DEBIT	BALANCE CREDIT

ACCOUNT ACCOUNT NO.

DATE		DESCRIPTION	POST. REF.	DEBIT	CREDIT	BALANCE DEBIT	BALANCE CREDIT

ACCOUNT ACCOUNT NO.

DATE		DESCRIPTION	POST. REF.	DEBIT	CREDIT	BALANCE DEBIT	BALANCE CREDIT

ACCOUNTS RECEIVABLE SUBSIDIARY LEDGER

NAME TERMS

DATE		DESCRIPTION	POST. REF.	DEBIT	CREDIT	BALANCE

NAME TERMS

DATE		DESCRIPTION	POST. REF.	DEBIT	CREDIT	BALANCE

 Name ______________________

ACCOUNTS RECEIVABLE SUBSIDIARY LEDGER

NAME ______________________ TERMS ______

DATE		DESCRIPTION	POST. REF.	DEBIT	CREDIT	BALANCE

NAME ______________________ TERMS ______

DATE		DESCRIPTION	POST. REF.	DEBIT	CREDIT	BALANCE

NAME ______________________ TERMS ______

DATE		DESCRIPTION	POST. REF.	DEBIT	CREDIT	BALANCE

NAME ______________________ TERMS ______

DATE		DESCRIPTION	POST. REF.	DEBIT	CREDIT	BALANCE

 Name

ACCOUNTS RECEIVABLE SUBSIDIARY LEDGER

NAME TERMS

DATE		DESCRIPTION	POST. REF.	DEBIT	CREDIT	BALANCE

ACCOUNTS PAYABLE SUBSIDIARY LEDGER

NAME TERMS

DATE		DESCRIPTION	POST. REF.	DEBIT	CREDIT	BALANCE

NAME TERMS

DATE		DESCRIPTION	POST. REF.	DEBIT	CREDIT	BALANCE

NAME TERMS

DATE		DESCRIPTION	POST. REF.	DEBIT	CREDIT	BALANCE

Name

MINI-PRACTICE SET 2 (continued)

Name ______________________________

	ACCOUNT NAME	TRIAL BALANCE DEBIT	TRIAL BALANCE CREDIT	ADJUSTMENTS DEBIT	ADJUSTMENTS CREDIT
1					
2					
3					
4					
5					
6					
7					
8					
9					
10					
11					
12					
13					
14					
15					
16					
17					
18					
19					
20					
21					
22					
23					
24					
25					
26					
27					
28					
29					
30					
31					
32					
33					
34					
35					
36					

 Name ____________________

ADJUSTED TRIAL BALANCE		INCOME STATEMENT		BALANCE SHEET		
DEBIT	CREDIT	DEBIT	CREDIT	DEBIT	CREDIT	
						1
						2
						3
						4
						5
						6
						7
						8
						9
						10
						11
						12
						13
						14
						15
						16
						17
						18
						19
						20
						21
						22
						23
						24
						25
						26
						27
						28
						29
						30
						31
						32
						33
						34
						35
						36

 Name

	ACCOUNT NAME	TRIAL BALANCE		ADJUSTMENTS	
		DEBIT	CREDIT	DEBIT	CREDIT
1					
2					
3					
4					
5					
6					
7					
8					
9					
10					
11					
12					
13					
14					
15					
16					
17					
18					
19					
20					
21					
22					
23					
24					
25					
26					
27					
28					
29					
30					
31					
32					
33					
34					
35					
36					

 Name ______________________

ADJUSTED TRIAL BALANCE		INCOME STATEMENT		BALANCE SHEET		
DEBIT	CREDIT	DEBIT	CREDIT	DEBIT	CREDIT	
						1
						2
						3
						4
						5
						6
						7
						8
						9
						10
						11
						12
						13
						14
						15
						16
						17
						18
						19
						20
						21
						22
						23
						24
						25
						26
						27
						28
						29
						30
						31
						32
						33
						34
						35
						36

 Name

 Name

MINI-PRACTICE SET 2 (continued)

Name ____________________

 Name

ACCOUNT NAME	DEBIT	CREDIT

 Name

EXTRA FORMS

	ACCOUNT NAME	TRIAL BALANCE DEBIT	TRIAL BALANCE CREDIT	ADJUSTMENTS DEBIT	ADJUSTMENTS CREDIT
1					
2					
3					
4					
5					
6					
7					
8					
9					
10					
11					
12					
13					
14					
15					
16					
17					
18					
19					
20					
21					
22					
23					
24					
25					
26					
27					
28					
29					
30					
31					
32					
33					
34					

 Name

ADJUSTED TRIAL BALANCE		INCOME STATEMENT		BALANCE SHEET		
DEBIT	CREDIT	DEBIT	CREDIT	DEBIT	CREDIT	
						1
						2
						3
						4
						5
						6
						7
						8
						9
						10
						11
						12
						13
						14
						15
						16
						17
						18
						19
						20
						21
						22
						23
						24
						25
						26
						27
						28
						29
						30
						31
						32
						33
						34

MINI-PRACTICE SET 2 (continued)

Name ______________________

EXTRA FORM

GENERAL JOURNAL

PAGE ______

DATE	DESCRIPTION	POST. REF.	DEBIT	CREDIT